The Power of Project Management Leadership

The Power of Project Management Leadership

Your Guide on How to Achieve Outstanding Results

LASZLO A. RETFALVI

CONTENTS

viii

DEDICATION

To my father-in-law,

Jamie Miller,

who lost his courageous fight with

cancer while I was writing this book.

He is the most outstanding Project Manager I have ever met.

A portion of proceeds from this book will be donated to the Canadian Cancer Society.

FOREWORD

In the last 50 years, project management has evolved from an expeditor and coordination role to the management of complex pieces, from system conception to design, integration, delivery, and long-term support. Along the way, methodologies, processes, and tools have been developed which, with the help of computer technology, have enabled improved planning, tracking, and control.

There has also been a proliferation in the number of project management how-to books published—most of them valuable, detailed guides that help project managers better plan and execute projects.

This book is different, however, and well overdue. It is about the Project Manager as an individual.

This book focuses on the important elements of management and leadership and on the careful balance between them in a project management environment. Much more importantly and uniquely, this book is a guide for achieving excellence as a Project Manager. It points the way forward to becoming what Laszlo refers to as an outstanding Project Manager.

In the course of my business career, I have worked with many Project Managers who could have benefited from the advice offered in this book. Indeed, I met few *outstanding* Project Managers during my many jobs in the Air Force and in business. And I was always aware that there was little written on the subject of leadership in project management.

For this reason, I was pleased when Laszlo asked me to help review drafts as he made progress with the book. While I contributed little to the messages in the book, I did become confident that the world of project management, and business in general, would be much better served as a result of the guidance in this book. I know that I could have used it during my project management days.

Laszlo has done an excellent job of capturing all of his thoughts pertaining to management and leadership—thoughts that he has garnered over the course of his career. He presents them, and a practical model, as a framework of the important components that lead to personal excellence in project management. The book explores how a risk-smart attitude and an accountability-based mindset are key components of leadership, and it relates these important ideas in the model for excellence.

Furthermore, Laszlo presents a self-evaluation guide to measure one's progress toward personal project management excellence. This is unique and will be of interest to seasoned Project Managers, people transitioning to project management, and those who are just starting a career in project management. Indeed, it will also be of interest to those who have general business management roles.

This book should soon find its way into MBA programs which, for too long, have ignored project management as a vital element of business.

Larry E. Johnson

Former President and Managing Director of General Dynamics UK Limited

INTRODUCTION

The subject of this book is how to create successful and outstanding Project Managers. Outstanding Project Managers are those who master project management leadership. Although I use the term Project Manager throughout the book, I do so mostly for convenience. I use the term broadly because the material in this book is not limited to Project Managers.

It is applicable to all project management roles and positions at all levels of project management. It also includes those individuals who support management activities, such as engineering managers, functional managers, as well as managers in operations, quality assurance, production, and commercial roles. It is also equally applicable to individuals managing programs and project portfolios. Basically, the term encompasses all individuals who interact with Project Managers as part of their work.

That is the beauty of this book. The content is relevant and can be applied whether you are a Project Manager, are supporting a Project Manager, or are starting out in the project management field. It is also of benefit to project teams as a whole.

So why did I write the book? It's time to get back to and remind ourselves of the basics. We need to focus on mastering them, as opposed to skipping them. We need to take time to reflect on and understand why certain individuals outperform others in the field of project management. I'm sure you've seen this in your day-to-day work.

Why are these individuals the "go-to" guys or gals we trust and admire? Why do these individuals get the best assignments and the best projects? Why are these individuals connected to senior and executive management and always receive the support they need? These are basic questions with not-so-simple answers—until now.

The goal of this book is to share with you the thoughts and experiences I've accumulated over the years, which will hopefully help you succeed and become the best at your game. To help you on your way, I have developed the Project Management Leadership Model as a framework and guide to help you better understand the basics.

The model emphasizes four areas that I believe are crucial to becoming an outstanding Project Manager: project management expertise, core leadership skills, a risk-smart attitude, and accountability-based behaviour. You cannot simply ignore, skip, or work around any of these areas. I will review each one and then explain how they interconnect.

The material also includes a very important assessment aspect. You will be able to assess your skills using the model and determine areas that may need improvement. I have also included a section with information to help you develop these areas.

I hope that you enjoy the material and that the application of the Project Management Leadership Model in your day-to-day activities will help you succeed and excel in your career.

Laszlo

CHAPTER 1: WHAT HAPPENED?

Very few initiatives today are so simple that they require little or no project management to guide them along. Those days are behind us. Today's projects require project management leadership to achieve success.

INTRODUCTION

You would think that with the abundance of project management training and the proliferation of various project management certifications, you would see a corresponding increase in project success. This does not appear to be the case. Almost every time I pick up a magazine or receive an e-mail, an organization or individual is promoting some type of training—different types of vendors promising mastery of a topic in a few short days. All these promotions, which I refer to as *silver bullets*, promise to help individuals become better Project Managers. Does that mean if you're trained or certified with one organization or another you must know what you're doing? I don't think so.

Please don't get me wrong. I am a firm believer in project management certification as a way of establishing yourself in your area of domain expertise. I, personally, hold the Province of Ontario Professional Engineer (P.Eng.) designation, the PMI® Project Management Professional (PMP) designation, and the PMI® Risk Management Professional (PMI-RMP) designation. Why? Because I believe in them. I believe and support their code of ethics, and I am passionate about the knowledge areas they represent.

But these alone do not give me the qualifications to become a recognized and successful Project Manager. They help, but there's much more involved. In the past, I have seen instances in which certification was the determining factor in whether or not an individual was selected, or perhaps hired, to become a Project Manager when, in fact, it should have been just *part* of the decision, not the *driver* of the decision. If you take time to research the prerequisites for a Project Manager position in your area, you'll see, more often than not, that some type of certification is required.

What I have found is that many Project Managers have not developed the right mix of skills and behaviours to be effective and successful. It almost seems that the technology and tools that we use today, such as e-mail or social media, are considered more important than the actual soft skills that Project Managers so dearly need.

In a way, these powerful tools cause us to skip or ignore the basics. As a result, our risk awareness suffers as we place our ability to listen effectively on the back burner. This lack of understanding of our current situation results in a significant lack of accountability.

So what happens when you mix all this together? You now have the perfect storm, in which the end result is that we would rather focus on what is easy, not what is important. This is a trap we must avoid. This is not project management.

The bottom line is that things need to change.

THERE HAS BEEN A SHIFT

We would all agree that most projects have undergone a drastic change over the last 10 to 15 years, or, in fact, even before that. There is probably no better example of this than the phenomenal growth of Information Technology (IT) projects and initiatives.

In the past, IT was merely an option for our projects. I remember working on projects and not having the ability to send e-mails. I used memos that were typed out and sent via interoffice mail. But in today's world, e-mail is no longer an optional tool. It has become the core of just about any activity or project that we do. In fact, many teams have moved passed this and now use Twitter (© Twitter Incorporated), Google+ (© Google Incorporated), or SharePoint (® Microsoft Corporation) as project communication tools. The IT industry has changed everything, and those who don't embrace it are simply left behind.

In today's competitive and fast-paced environment, what we need to be able to do effectively is to deliver high-quality products, projects, and services at competitive prices. Remaining competitive is critical to an organization's survival. Very few of us have the luxury of sitting back and letting customers come to us. We need to go to them armed with the best product, project solution, or service available. Otherwise, they will simply go somewhere else to get what they need. The end result is that we may find ourselves in the unemployment line.

Project Managers have it pretty tough. They face many challenges and hardships in successfully delivering the best product, project solution, or service. These challenges include such things as:

- Tighter budgets which, because of increased customer expectations and all these new software tools, tend to be much more heavily monitored and scrutinized.
- Much shorter implementation schedules on traditional projects than ever before. For example, an IT installation and training project may now take only two months to complete. That's lightning fast compared to larger projects that require years of work. The project may be started and finished even before it is properly set up in the organization's financial reporting system.
- Global teams with varying and, at times, conflicting cultures and practices. With global teams comes the required management of those teams. Most people do not realize the burden this places on a Project Manager.
- Countless tools and software applications, each promising to be the silver bullet that will help us make the management of our projects easier. Although these tools can be beneficial, Project Managers need to consider them very carefully and determine which ones they truly need. Tools do not replace leadership.
- A project's impact on end users. For example, a small software update of a security feature in a large, global organization may impact thousands of users.

- Daily flood of e-mails and instant communications in which everybody considers their message to be the most important and expects an immediate response.
- Instantaneous reports showing progress against requirements, schedules, cost—you name it. What previously took weeks of effort compiling documents can now be done in, literally, a few hours or less.

When you pull all these factors together, Project Managers now also face the serious challenge of effectively implementing time management for their daily activities—no easy task.

Clearly, things have changed significantly. Project management has moved from the old-fashioned paper and charts pinned up on the wall to instantaneous communications, agile methodologies, Scrum Masters, sophisticated software-based decision tools, and cloud-based computing. I remember managing and being involved in projects where we did everything on the wall with yellow sticky notes. Nowadays, I find that we are slowly reverting back to similar techniques while calling them by a different name. Why? Because they're proven, and they work.

So what has happened to Project Managers in all of this? In certain ways, unfortunately, Project Managers have been left behind. They are overwhelmed and are struggling to keep up. The more they work, the more work they have to do. I have found that organizations tend to be dishonest with themselves by almost always underestimating the complexity of a new initiative or the need for a Project Manager. As a result, Project Managers are, more and more often, hiding behind their work by placing spins on reports that they produce thanks to those tools we just talked about. Why do we see the cliff and let the Project Manager run for it and jump?

In my experience, many Project Managers have not developed the right mix of skills and behaviours to be successful. Project Managers need to realize that standards, methodologies, and the sexy tools available today improve their performance only to a certain extent. They are not the answer to everything. They are not silver bullets.

It is far better to have a strong Project Manager who uses yellow sticky notes on the wall than a weak Project Manager who uses the best processes and tools available. Ultimately, it's all about understanding the goal and getting the job done with minimal risk.

So what do we need to do? We need to get off the train and re-educate ourselves on the basics.

EMBRACING CHANGE

Although we have made great advancements in project management—and please don't get me wrong, improved methodologies and tools are great—we have also created a serious issue. In all this, we have forgotten what makes a Project Manager excel in his or her field. I refer to such individuals as *outstanding Project Managers.*

We need to take advantage of all these great advancements, but we need to do so carefully and with tact. We need to wrap around these advancements the skills required to use them effectively. We need to understand what these advancements offer and how they work before we can run off and implement the latest ones. As you'll see, most of them impact the Project Manager in one way or another.

My example in this case is agile project management. During my risk management activities, I had the opportunity to study the agile approach and methodology. Quite frankly, what it offers we should already be doing. In fact, most of us have been doing it. The only difference is that now we have something to call it. One point that always makes me smile is that agile (more specifically, Scrum, which is a form of agile) requires daily meetings. Imagine that: meeting daily to understand progress and issues. Another requirement is frequent communication with the customer as well as making the customer part of the team. Wow. It sounds impressive even though it's not. Shouldn't we already be doing this?

Nonetheless, I took an initiative to investigate and to learn. I attended conferences on agile project management to gain insight. I even presented to industry on the subject. And you know what? It does offer advantages, some of which include emphasis on business value and overall agility. These resonate strongly with leadership, risk management, and accountability. Interestingly enough, though, I have not embraced the agile methodology formally as a whole. I have, however, embraced agile as an improved method for leading teams and addressing risks. Being agile in terms of style and approach is very powerful.

The point is that change is inevitable. It cannot be avoided. You have to accept it and go with it. The winner is the one who recognizes change and embraces it while not forgetting the basics. The key to successful project management is to understand this and build on it.

We all face the same struggles: full days, busy schedules, staffing challenges, milestones and deadlines to meet, urgent issues to address, and fires to put out. From my experience, with all this going on, Project Managers tend to lose focus. They forget about the basics required to be successful at their jobs.

This is where tackling bad habits and the Project Management Leadership Model come in.

BREAK AWAY FROM YOUR BAD HABITS

Habits are things that we do without really thinking about why we do them. We all have habits. Take a moment to think about any bad habits you may have. At the same time, think about your good habits. Focus on these—single them out and keep improving on them. Change the ones that aren't so good. A great exercise for you to try is to create a list with two columns: one for your good habits and one for your bad habits. In most cases, the bad habits will outnumber the good habits.

Most Project Managers also have bad habits. These bad habits include things like working around established processes and procedures because they might slow down or add an extra expense to the project. Another common bad habit is not paying adequate attention to spelling in e-mails. I'd like to share with you how I feel about this last example. If my name is incorrectly spelled in an e-mail, I will not answer it. It tells me how much attention to detail the sender has put into the message. If the e-mail is not important enough to deserve getting my name right, then obviously it is not important enough to respond to.

Review the next few examples and see if you can relate.

Have you ever caught yourself micromanaging when, in fact, it wasn't necessary? While there are times when you do have to micromanage (because you have to help out in a critical situation or take a deep dive because a team member is not around), micromanaging on a regular basis is something that you, as a Project Manager, need to steer clear of. Let your team handle the details.

Do you try to avoid conflict by not voicing your opinion on a tough issue? How about managing by *not* walking around or reaching out? How about keeping important information to yourself instead of sharing it openly?

Do you use the word *I* in the context of project work (as opposed to my use of *I* as "I am writing this book")? How many Project Managers you know use of the word *I*? In the project team, it's not about *I*—it's about *we*. Some Project Managers operate alone or in a matrix organization. The same rule applies. Keep the focus off yourself as best as you can.

Do you start each day without a well-thought-out and prioritized action plan? You are not alone. Usually, Project Managers come to the office, turn on their computers, and just go. E-mails are already waiting for them, and important things do not get done. You have to think out your day before you start it.

Do you find yourself not listening to your colleagues and downplaying risks just because they may entail more work? How about avoiding accountability?

As Project Managers, we all have bad habits in some shape or form, and the above-mentioned examples are just a few of the most common ones I've come across. I'm sure there are more. But from this, it's obvious to see that we need to do something to move forward. But *what*?

We cannot stand still, but at the same time, we cannot lose focus of the basics. We need to build on the basics, not shy away from them. In my career, I needed a framework to fall back on as a simple reminder of the basics. This is actually how the Project Management Leadership Model was born and refined. I watched other people's behaviours and what they did. I worked alongside outstanding Project Managers and excellent leaders, and I took note of their good habits. I paid close attention to advice I got from my mentors.

The model, which we will review in detail, is meant to act as a reminder of and guide to the basics that we need to master to become outstanding Project Managers. By studying and implementing the model, you will very quickly be able to identify your bad habits, to challenge these head on, and to develop the necessary good habits to excel in your career.

HOW THE MODEL WILL HELP YOU SUCCEED

The Project Manager Leadership Model is all about focus. It's about focusing on what is important, not what is easy. Easy is what our bad habits represent. The model comprises four key components:

- Project management expertise
- Core leadership skills
- Risk-smart attitude
- Accountability-based behaviour

Each of these areas significantly contributes to your success. The components are also interlinked—you cannot be an outstanding Project Manager unless you master these four areas. Similarly, you cannot be an outstanding Project Manager without being aware of and actively implementing all four areas at any given time. The approach is not singular; all of these things must be implemented at the same time.

So why do most individuals and Project Managers fail to see this? Is it because it's something new? Or is it something particularly unique? No, on both counts.

Then why? The truth is that we have let ourselves step away from the basics because sticking to them requires dedication and hard work. It may expose problems and reveal underachievement. Let's face it, nobody wants be singled out as a weak performer.

But this is not the intent of the model. The model helps you to understand the basics that must be mastered before you can become an outstanding Project Manager.

PREPARE TO UNLEASH THE POWER OF PROJECT MANAGEMENT LEADERSHIP

So how do you do this? First of all, you need to review and understand the material in this book, which I intentionally wrote in a candid, casual, and conversational tone. It's an easy read with each chapter addressing one of the core components of the Project Management Leadership Model. At the end, I will discuss how to pull all the information together so that you can move forward.

You also need to review and compare your reality to the material itself. I have created a Project Management Leadership Assessment (see Chapter 8) to assist you with this. You are encouraged to complete this detailed assessment once you have covered the material. It allows you to identify any gaps in your skills—and we all have varying levels of gaps in our skills. This is something that we have to recognize, acknowledge, and work on honestly. Even the areas that we feel we excel in should be considered so that we may continue to excel.

Once you have identified gaps in your skills, you can develop an action plan to bridge these gaps using the tips and techniques provided in Chapter 9 or, perhaps, using your own. Once you have completed this section, you can apply the newly learned knowledge and skills, and monitor your performance as well as your path to becoming an outstanding Project Manager.

KEY CHAPTER TAKE-AWAYS

- Many Project Managers have not developed the right mix of skills and behaviours to be successful.

- We need to break away from our bad habits as they cloud and impede self-improvement.

- The following four components result in successful project management leadership:

  o Project management expertise

  o Core leadership skills

  o Risk-smart attitude

  o Accountability-based behaviour

- The Project Management Leadership Model integrates these components and provides a framework to help you become a highly competent and outstanding Project Manager.

CHAPTER 2: THE PROJECT MANAGEMENT LEADERSHIP MODEL

It takes true project management leadership to successfully drive today's aggressive and complex projects. This includes a significant emphasis on risk and accountability.

INTRODUCTION

Project Managers need to understand that management is not the same as leadership. Typically, these terms are used interchangeably and, most of time, incorrectly. Management and leadership are *not* the same. In fact, they are opposites, and this is where most issues begin.

Management is the ability to get the job done while leadership refers to having a vision, sharing the vision with the team, and then setting the course to achieve the vision. Project management leadership combines both of these skills together to lay the foundation of outstanding Project Managers.

Project management leadership combines select project management and leadership skills with a risk-smart attitude and accountability. Why are these last two behaviours emphasized? Because they are very important. These two areas make such a difference in the performance of Project Managers that they need to be called out separately.

PROJECT MANAGEMENT LEADERSHIP MODEL

Project management leadership, by itself, is a powerful juxtaposition of two terms: project management and leadership. As mentioned earlier, you need both to succeed in today's aggressive project world.

The Project Management Leadership Model raises the bar even higher. It comprises four key components—project management expertise, core leadership skills, a risk-smart attitude, and accountability-based behaviour—with emphasis placed on the last two. These two areas are so important that they are front and centre in the model. And while one could argue that being risk-smart and being accountable are elements of core leadership, I disagree. Putting emphasis on these two areas individually provides a new context for their meaning and intent.

In my experience, a risk-smart attitude and accountability-based behaviour are game changers. They catapult your performance to a new level and set the important groundwork for becoming an outstanding Project Manager.

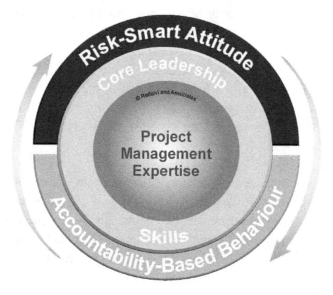

Figure 2.1. Project Management Leadership Model.

Each of the four key components of the model has a number of subcomponents, or attributes. Figure 2.1 shows the model as a diagram. We will discuss the four main components in the following sections and the attributes of each component later on in individual chapters.

Now, let's review the purpose of the arrows on the perimeter of the model. They are there to remind you that the model is iterative, focused on improving your performance over time. You need to work on the components and attributes of the model continually. Never stand still, and always aim to improve your skills. Just as the environment around you changes, you have to change if you want to stay on top of your game.

PROJECT MANAGEMENT EXPERTISE

Project Managers plan, manage, and handle details in a way that lets others relax. Project management expertise is, therefore, about having the skills to develop a plan and manage that plan. It's about getting things done and delivering. It's about meeting milestones and deadlines. It requires structure. It involves some type of process. Depending on your location and your business, you likely have access to a number of different standards and methodologies to help you with this process. And at the end of the day, all Project Managers have the same goal: the successful delivery of a project.

Now that you know that project management expertise is a core component of the Project Management Leadership Model, you may be wondering exactly which project management skills make up this expertise? We will discuss this in detail later on, but in brief, they include such key items as understanding the big picture, planning, and scheduling.

CORE LEADERSHIP SKILLS

Leadership is about having a vision and being able to motivate individuals to share and act on that vision. It's about establishing direction and inspiring others to follow that direction. Both of these are very difficult tasks because they're all about people, and everyone is different. You need to know how to interact with people so that they will want to help you turn your vision into a reality.

Leadership is about navigating through change and adopting a forward-looking stance. You have to be thinking ahead constantly because you want to get to something important. Unlike a project that requires us to get somewhere because we have deliverables, leadership is much more forward-looking.

Individuals follow leaders because they want to, not because they have to. Generally, staff members look up to and follow Project Managers because they *have* to. They do the tasks they are instructed to do, but that's it. If you want them to follow you whole-heartedly, you have to earn their trust and confidence. This further amplifies the importance of being a leader with a compelling vision.

In today's world, project management expertise needs to be supplemented with core leadership skills—the two must work together simultaneously. This is partly due to the ever-changing nature of projects and how they fit with strategic initiatives. Organizations that stand still will not succeed. Change demands leadership.

RISK-SMART ATTITUDE

This component is very close to my heart because it is one of the areas of project management that I really enjoy. Having a risk-smart attitude can significantly increase your probability of success.

Individuals frequently ask me what I mean by *risk-smart*. What is involved in having a risk-smart attitude? Well, being risk-smart is about constantly being aware of threats or opportunities around you. This is a key point because risks may also be opportunities, and as such, you need to develop a different mindset if you want to be able to recognize them. People perceive risk management as a way to deal with threats, but it can also be a powerful tool that helps us identify opportunities. You need to actively try to balance or offset threats with opportunities. Furthermore, when you are making a decision, you should have a very good understanding of the implications of that decision ahead of time.

A risk-smart attitude is about awareness, and it's a key component of success. When dealing with risk, you have to be risk-smart by understanding threats, opportunities, and risk attitudes.

Having a risk-smart attitude is all about setting things up for success at the start. It's not about being reactionary, but rather, about looking forward. This is not to say that you don't need to review and, perhaps, adjust your project plan as you execute it—this should be done constantly.

A risk-smart attitude is not about being averse to risks, and it's not about seeking risks. It's about carefully managing the balance between the two, being aware of the risks that are around you at all times, and understanding how others view these risks.

ACCOUNTABILITY-BASED BEHAVIOUR

Accountability is one of those terms that are not well understood by Project Managers and most individuals. Accountability is defined as a willingness to accept responsibility for something that you have done or something that you're supposed to do. It is very different from responsibility. Being responsible does not make you accountable. An individual may be responsible without feeling accountable. The key here is to make sure that the things you're supposed to do tie in with something beneficial to the project's success. There is project value associated with accountability.

Accountability involves believing in yourself so that others will believe in you. Take a moment to reflect on this. Do you consistently act in an accountable manner? When people come by and ask you for help, do you help them? Do the individuals around you know that you care, follow through, and can be consistently counted on?

Accountability is the foundation of project management leadership, and it's a key ingredient in implementing change. It's about setting and meeting expectations and accepting the consequences of not meeting those expectations.

This is the type of accountability-based behaviour we need from Project Managers. It's about going the extra mile. It's not about playing any blame games. You do not blame anybody else for the situation—you recognize shortfalls and work through them. It's all about helping others even though your helping others may not directly help you. The importance of accountability cannot be emphasized enough.

PULLING IT ALL TOGETHER

Now that we've identified the four components of the Project Management Leadership Model, how do we pull all of them together so that we may benefit from them?

Let's follow the general approach identified in Figure 2.2. We will review each component and its attributes, determine any gaps that require improvement, review tips and techniques that may help, and work to close these gaps in order to become outstanding Project Managers.

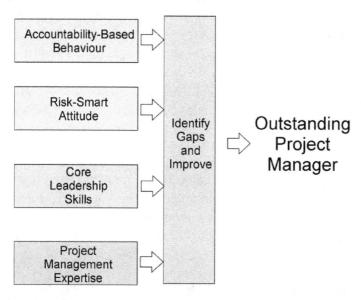

Figure 2.2. Project Management Leadership Model—Process.

To better understand this process, we will review each component separately and go into more depth as we progress through the book. Understanding the components in more detail will help you better understand how each component and its attributes contribute to you being an outstanding Project Manager.

The key to achieving success with this model is to integrate all four components while ensuring balance between them. Although each individual component plays an important part in the model, the interaction between all the components is what makes the biggest difference. *All four components must be in play at the same time if you want to be an outstanding Project Manager*. It can thus be said that the sum of the components is far greater than the individual components on their own. When all of the *attributes work together*, the model exhibits a multiplier effect over each individual attribute.

MAKING THE MODEL WORK FOR YOU

Now that we've had an overview of the model, what's next? Before we go any further, please take time to review your current activities and attempt to align them with each component. Do a quick assessment, and identify any major gaps by performing an honest initial assessment based on your current knowledge of the four components. Use Figure 2.3 to rate yourself as weak, average, or strong. Do not worry at this point about the exact definitions of weak, average, and strong. This is meant to be a quick assessment only. You will have the opportunity to do a more detailed assessment later on, once we review the complete model.

Component	Initial Assessment		
Project management expertise	Weak	Average	Strong
Core leadership skills	Weak	Average	Strong
Risk-smart attitude	Weak	Average	Strong
Accountability-based behaviour	Weak	Average	Strong

Figure 2.3. Project Management Leadership Model—Initial Assessment.

The next step is to ask a colleague (or, better yet, your supervisor) to perform the same initial assessment of you. How did you do? Were the two assessments similar or were they different? Which areas were similar or different?

The key thing to get from this initial assessment is that what you think of yourself may be significantly different than what others think of you. Having encountered this over and over again, especially early on in my career when I was evaluated using similar models, I was always amazed by the fact that what I thought of myself wasn't the same as what other people saw. In some cases, it was radically different.

One of things I found frustrating in my project management career is that many organizations struggle with defining observable leadership behaviours that are expected from a Project Manager. Perhaps you have experienced the same problem within your organization. Upon reflection, I realized that what was missing in all this was a concise and consistent approach for the assessment of Project Manager performance—one that would show Project Managers what they really needed to focus on.

This is where the Project Management Leadership Model comes into play. It identifies the areas that are needed as well as the areas that you need to improve upon. It provides a common playing field in the area of project management leadership.

Once you have completed this exercise, keep both initial assessments nearby for future reference. We will review this initial assessment in Chapter 8, which contains a detailed assessment using the Project Management Leadership Model. You are encouraged to complete that assessment once I have reviewed the entire model with you.

Honesty is key if you want the model to be of benefit to you—honesty about how you believe you rank against these components and their individual attributes. You need to understand this clearly before you can go on to develop a plan for getting better at individual items. It's all about learning and being aware of what is needed. Work on it. This won't be easy. It will need dedication and commitment, but it will be well worth it.

SO WHAT?

If you want to remain a mediocre Project Manager, and you're satisfied with your current performance, this book is not for you. This book is meant to help you get better at what you do as a Project Manager, guiding you along your way to becoming an outstanding Project Manager.

If you are new to project management, are happy with your current status quo, and do not want to learn how to excel, this book is also not for you. It's unfortunate because sooner or later you will find yourself at a huge disadvantage but, by your choice, this book is not for you.

If you want to succeed and become an outstanding Project Manager—the go-to guy or gal we mentioned earlier—learn to apply the material in this book regardless of your current level of expertise or how much experience you have. Project management is not an easy field to master. It's not about sitting behind a desk tapping out e-mails on your computer, sending them to others, and hoping for the best. It can be quite stressful and, from my experience, Project Managers need all the help they can get in today's complex world.

The Project Management Leadership Model gives you a solid framework to work with—it's practical and straightforward, and it can be applied immediately in your day-to-day activities. The model's four components and their attributes will help you with your work, putting you in a much better position with your staff, supervisor, management, customers, and stakeholders. You will develop a sense of pride and recognition that you will cherish for a long time to come.

As I always say, "I'd rather be the hammer than the nail."

PROJECT MANAGEMENT LEADERSHIP MODEL—DO'S AND DON'TS

Do's

- Be honest with yourself. Do you want to succeed? Do you want to become an outstanding Project Manager? If so, are you willing to invest the time required to make this happen?

- Ensure you do an honest initial ranking of yourself against the four major components to identify any major gaps. We will work on how to close the gaps as we progress.

- Find a buddy or a coach to accompany you on this journey—you can bounce ideas off each other, and, in this way, you can both improve.

- Ask questions. You are not alone on this journey, and others want you to succeed. Reaching out for help from your peers and colleagues is a strength, not a weakness.

Don'ts

- Don't rush this. Mastering the model does not occur overnight. It requires effort, practice, and feedback. Rest assured—the time spent on this is well worth it.

- Don't jump around from chapter to chapter. It's best to read the book in the sequence it is written.

- Don't focus on just the components that interest you. True success is in the understanding and integration of all components and their attributes.

- Don't put this book down—you will regret it!

KEY CHAPTER TAKE-AWAYS

- Project Managers need to understand that management of projects is not the same as leadership of projects.

- The secret is that both project management and leadership are necessary for success in today's ever-changing business environment.

- It takes true project management leadership to successfully drive today's aggressive and complex projects.

- Although each component of the Project Management Leadership Model is critical on its own, it's the integration and interaction of all four components—project management expertise, core leadership skills, a risk-smart attitude, and accountability-based behaviour—that makes the model unique and effective.

- If you want to succeed and become an outstanding Project Manager, learn to apply the material in this book in your day-to-day activities regardless of your current level of expertise or how much experience you have.

CHAPTER 3: PROJECT MANAGEMENT EXPERTISE

Project Managers plan, manage, and handle project details in a way that helps stakeholders relax. Good Project Managers are hard to find, and outstanding Project Managers are rarer still.

INTRODUCTION

To properly understand the term *project management*, it is of benefit to understand what it's based on. *Management* stems from the Latin *manu agere,* which means "to lead by the hand." Management is one of those terms that is so broadly applied that it has become an accepted daily activity. No matter what we do, we barely make it through a day without managing something.

In its simplest form, management is about the process of leading and directing all or part of an organization or group of people through the use of proper resources. General management skills are skills that a manager needs in order to manage any undertaking. These general management skills are the foundation of project management.

A manager is responsible for planning and directing the work of a group of individuals, monitoring their work, and taking corrective action when necessary. A manager's title generally reflects what he or she is responsible for. For example, an Operations Manager is responsible for the operations of an organization. A Quality Manager is responsible for the quality activities of an organization. There are many different management functions in business, and I'm sure that you, too, can name a few. Regardless of the title, however, a manager is still responsible for planning, directing, monitoring, and controlling people in their work.

Project management, in contrast, is generally understood as the discipline of planning, organizing, securing, and managing resources to achieve specific project goals. The PMI® Project Management Book of Knowledge (PMBOK ®) defines project management as "the application of knowledge, skills, tools, and techniques to project activities to meet project requirements." A Project Manager is, therefore, a person whose overall responsibility is to successfully plan, execute, and deliver a project. This can be a pretty significant undertaking.

The Project Manager title is used in construction, oil, defence, pharmaceutical, telecom, aerospace, information technology, and many other industries that produce products, systems, and services. With so many different types of Project Managers, what makes you a better Project Manager; better than the rest? Part of the secret is how you master project management expertise.

WHAT IS PROJECT MANAGEMENT EXPERTISE?

What is project management expertise? What is so unique about it? What do you, as a Project Manager, have that other Project Managers don't? Well, in short, project management expertise is the basis of credibility of a person who is perceived to be knowledgeable in project management. This knowledge is formed by a combination of his or her education, training, and experience. To be an outstanding Project Manager, you need to master key project management attributes.

I'm sure you've run into Project Managers who have had more skills, knowledge, and management abilities than others. Project management skills vary by industry, but they are bound by a common set of attributes. For example, Project Managers in the construction industry need some of the same attributes as Project Managers in the telecom industry. Only the specifics of the business sector vary. The bottom line is that it's all about being very good at what you do, no matter what field or business sector you are in. This is what project management expertise refers to.

It is also about your reputation, and your reputation should at all times be positive. Take a moment and reflect: have you ever worked with a Project Manager who you did not like being associated with? Why is this? Perhaps it's because that person had a reputation for being overly tough or for not managing activities properly. Or maybe that person was known to manage by bullying or, perhaps, to be overly negative.

All of us have had our experiences, but what should really be coming to the forefront is the realization that your reputation always comes first—you have a much greater opportunity to succeed if your reputation is positive. If you have a good reputation, people will *want* to work with you instead of *having* to work with you.

Project management expertise includes relevant experience. You must have relevant experience in order to have the expertise. You have to go through many different projects, learn your lessons, and earn the scars from which you will grow.

One thing that I quickly learned as a consultant is that you never offer services that you have not mastered. This also applies to Project Managers within any organization. There are times—and this happens more frequently than not—when Project Managers state that they can do something when, in fact, they have no experience doing it. Luckily, I have come to understand that you should not lead people on like this as the consequences, particularly in a project environment, may be severe. You have to do things a first time to learn.

Growth in expertise is different from assuming expertise. This is why we have different levels of project management seniority and maturity in organizations. Experience, which generally goes from junior to the most senior levels, is also taken into account, and it's where project management expertise comes into play.

WHY IS PROJECT MANAGEMENT EXPERTISE IMPORTANT?

For those of us who have worked on numerous projects, it doesn't take long to recognize if a project is being managed well or poorly. In general, poorly managed projects are not successful and result in schedule delays, increased costs, and overall angst. This is usually a reflection of your skills and experience as a Project Manager. It also results in both disappointed stakeholders and disappointed customers. Depending on the situation, you may get removed, reassigned, or even fired.

Project Managers need to have a clear understanding of how various project areas integrate and interact with each other. Project Managers are authorized on behalf of the organization to execute a project. This must not be taken lightly—it's a big deal! As such, you need to be on top of your game.

Project Managers are selected to do an important job, and that job is the successful delivery of a project. It cannot occur unless there is a certain level of project management expertise, otherwise the project was either too easy or you got lucky, and chances are that you won't be that lucky again in future projects.

Remember that, at the end of the day, most organizations need to return a profit. To do so, projects have to be executed effectively and efficiently. Bad project management erodes the profit margin of any organization. Most projects today are complex and clearly require properly trained and experienced Project Managers to manage them. The consequences of not properly executing the project may be quite severe for the overall organization.

The best offence is a good defence, and in this case, that's project management expertise.

PROJECT MANAGEMENT EXPERTISE—ATTRIBUTES YOU NEED TO MASTER

As I mentioned earlier, all Project Managers need to master key project management attributes, which, when combined, are known as project management expertise. In the past—and I'm sure this will continue into the future—my colleagues and I have had many heated discussions about what these project management attributes should be. There are literally hundreds of books on project management skills available on the market (feel free to do your own research). However, there's no definite answer.

To help with this, the Project Management Leadership Model includes the attributes that I consider to be the most important based on my past experiences. Some of you may argue that a list like this is incomplete or, perhaps, oversimplified. Nonetheless, there is no doubt in my mind that these items, which I will be discussing later on in this chapter, are the most critical to your success. Are there others? Possibly, but the ones listed here apply to *all* Project Managers and *all* projects, *all* of the time.

So what happens if you do not have these skills? Do you give up being a Project Manager and find a new career? Of course not— although a nice job in Florida, running a deep-sea fishing business does sound enticing. The intent of all of this is to identify these attributes and explain what they are so that you can take steps to improve on them.

With that said, the first step is to recognize your weaknesses and take the initiative to learn.

UNDERSTAND THE BIG PICTURE

Imagine this. You've just had a project assigned to you, and you've been asked to brief project stakeholders and management on your progress. Do you struggle with your ability to explain the project in simple and clear terms?

It has been my experience that the majority of Project Managers cannot easily explain their project. They tend to go into useless details when stakeholders just want to get a high-level description of what the project is about, what the key items to be accomplished are, and what the overall schedule and costs are.

Successful Project Managers are valued for their ability to balance an understanding of the big picture, which is the overall aim of the project, with the many smaller tasks that comprise the project. You need to understand how the project that you are executing fits in with the bigger picture of your organization especially in terms of strategy, finances, operations, and business risks.

Before taking on any project, you need to understand what the project is all about. Ask yourself, how does it fit in with the big scheme of things in my organization? Does the project fall under a program I should be aware of? Is the project a key strategic component of the organization?

You need to have a clear understanding of customer and stakeholder priorities. You need to keep your project team focused on the big picture while not losing sight of important details. Think about how you, at a high level, are going to complete this project successfully. It's not about detail planning. Not at all. It's about understanding the project DNA from a top-level point of view—a view commonly referred to as *a 30,000-foot view*.

You need to identify who the real customer is and come to an agreement with him or her about what constitutes a successful project conclusion. This successful conclusion also needs to be shared with and approved by senior management.

Ask yourself, does the project make sense? Is the team aware of all the stakeholders? Has this or something very similar ever been done before in the organization? Do we understand the high-level project deliverables? Next, think about how the project will be accomplished. Who is the end customer? Do you understand the high-level risks?

Your ability to see the big picture puts your project in context. It helps you and your team operate more efficiently because you understand the project. It helps you see what is important to the project and to your stakeholders.

Ask yourself, can I explain my project simply on one page and, if not, why not? The one thing to remember when you're explaining your project is to avoid going into too much detail, hand-waving, and waffling. Learn to get to the message across quickly, otherwise, there is a good chance that the project will be delayed, assigned to a new

Project Manager, or even cancelled as it appears too disorganized and risky.

RECOGNIZE A GOOD REQUIREMENT FROM A BAD ONE

A common problem that a large number of Project Managers run into is that they accept projects or become Project Managers of projects that have poorly written requirements. That can be a tough, no-win situation. A major challenge for you and your staff is recognizing a well-written requirement from a poor one. Take time to reflect on this. Consider projects you have worked on in the past or, perhaps, one you are currently working on. Do you have a solid set of requirements? If not, what do you plan to do about it?

Poorly written project requirements represent risk. They represent potential scope creep, change in project scope. As such, they need to be addressed head on—the sooner the better. As a Project Manager, you need to determine what is in and what is out. This may sound easy, but it's not.

Most project issues occur due to poorly articulated project requirements, in terms of both documentation and communication. As a result, team members and stakeholders have different interpretations of what needs to be done. Poor requirements are like a trap that says, "Got ya, now deliver!" Customers will always have something over you when you have weak requirements unless you address them properly and promptly.

How can you develop a project plan without understanding the requirements? My agilista colleagues claim that this is what their approach is trying to address. Regardless of this, and regardless of the project, you still need to properly understand, frame, and articulate requirements along the way and then work from there. As we discussed earlier, you have to understand the big picture.

Proper requirements must be realistic, clearly articulated, understood by all stakeholders, and prioritized. Let's say you have 100 project requirements. Usually, some will trump others. When it comes to managing requirements, the best approach is to sit down with the key stakeholders (the priority being the customer) and ask them which requirements are most important to deliver first in case you run into difficulties. This does not relieve you of your duty to deliver the project in its entirety, but at least you know that there is a priority in terms of what the stakeholders want and expect. This helps you identify risks and focus on what is important. What's more, it increases your chances of customer satisfaction if difficulties do arise.

A frequently forgotten aspect of setting proper requirements is that they must be verifiable. How do you know that your team has met a requirement if you cannot verify it? Do you inspect it? Do you test it? If a requirement is written in a manner that is not verifiable, then it is not a properly written requirement.

One of the worst requirement offences, if there is such a thing, is ambiguity. Generating a requirement that is not clear and succinct does not help the project. It actually hurts it because you now need to spend time and energy figuring out what the requirement is all about. If there are two or more possible interpretations of a requirement, the requirement is ambiguous. You need to be able to recognize this trap.

You should also keep an eye out for any assumptions and constraints associated with requirements. Basically, do not make assumptions! And if you do make assumptions, make sure that they are clearly documented and understood by all project stakeholders. The same applies to any constraints associated with a requirement. Understand your constraints. Make sure that these are clearly documented, understood, and agreed to by all stakeholders.

Generating proper project requirements is difficult, and it takes practice. Do not underestimate the effort required, and do not rush this step, otherwise you may end up in the bad requirements trap and have a very difficult time getting out.

BE ABLE TO ANALYZE AND BREAK DOWN PROBLEMS

Have you ever been assigned a challenging project that had a very complex technical or commercial problem and when you tried to explain it, you had a very difficult time doing so? You are not alone. What greatly helps in these situations is the ability to break down a problem into smaller, more comprehensible, chunks. Why? Because it's about understanding what you're trying to accomplish. You need to break down problems into smaller chunks and work on the chunks separately.

Problem reduction and problem-solving are fundamental in a Project Manager's role. Your ability to take a complex problem, issue, or risk and break it down so that both you and others clearly understand it is key. Systematically breaking down a tough problem into manageable chunks greatly increases the probability of project success.

However, you need to be careful here. You may understand the problem, but the real proof of success is when others understand it as well. And as project complexity increases, this ability to analyze and break down problems becomes even more relevant. If you cannot break down a problem properly, you cannot explain it. If you cannot break down a problem properly, you cannot create a plan for it. If you cannot break down a problem properly, you cannot execute and solve it. The bottom line is that your inability to break down a problem properly means that you have missed three key steps in project management.

A hidden or unsolved problem exposes your project and organization to risk. This is what occurs when you just skim over it, hoping that it will go away. In reality, you should make every effort to define major problems early on in the project and break them down into manageable chunks as soon as possible. We all know this, but we tend to forget it. Why? Because it is a hard thing to do. Project Managers tend to focus on low-hanging fruit first so that they can show progress.

Before you take any action, you must first properly define the problem. This is a very important step because it sets the tone for how

31

you plan to meet the requirements of the project. The approach to breaking down a problem is systematic; it's done using established systems engineering principles.

Your breakdown has to be performed in the correct order to minimize wasted time and maximize the use of valuable project resources. You need to ensure that you and your team are breaking down problems and developing proper solutions, not spending your efforts on the background or origin of the problem. That will come later. For now, focus on what is important, not the low-hanging fruit.

KNOW HOW TO PLAN

The ability to properly plan a project is an attribute of project management expertise that is difficult and yet absolutely critical to success. Planning is not scheduling—avoid this misconception. Planning is about seeing the big picture and developing a credible approach that will allow you to execute and complete your project successfully.

Scheduling comes after planning, and this is where time and resource loading components come into play. Unfortunately, today's scheduling tools make it easy to skip crucial planning tasks and get into scheduling details way too early. You must avoid making a scheduling "deep dive" too soon even though it can be very easy to do so with available scheduling tools.

Planning is an art that you need to master. Certain individuals are better at planning than others because they have had the practice. They also understand the bigger picture. They can take the bigger picture, break it down into manageable chunks, and identify major issues and risks that need to be addressed. All these steps are necessary in coming up with a credible plan. A simple way to get started is to ask yourself and your team, have we done this project before? If so, how did we do it?

Planning is all about identifying the tasks that you need to do. This includes sequencing and recognizing interdependencies. You need to master the use of work breakdown structures to understand the basics of proper project planning.

Planning involves understanding the scope, the required resources, and the deliverables of a project. Projects are generally seen as failures when they do not produce the expected deliverables. The same analogy applies to you as a Project Manager. You must only plan and promise what you can deliver, and then go on and deliver it. It sounds easy, but real-life experience shows the opposite.

Planning is difficult. Planning requires reflection, discussion, consultation, and focus. It requires practice. Ensure that you are outcome-driven, that you focus on business results, and that you do what you said you were going to do. You will increase your probability of planning success.

Planning methods such as mind maps or decision trees, which help you understand relationships between project ideas, are an excellent approach to project planning. A clear understanding of how to develop project network diagrams is also required. Network diagrams allow us to see the relationships between project activities and project constraints, and they're particularly useful in visualizing critical or complex areas of your project plan. Network diagrams are also the basis upon which scheduling tools construct project schedules.

Without a clearly understood and worked-out plan of your project, it will be very difficult for you to create a realistic schedule. This will result in an increased likelihood of schedule rework, a waste of precious project resources, and increased costs. You need to work hard to avoid this kind of situation, otherwise your management may end up giving you unwanted help.

EXCEL AT SCHEDULING

We've talked about understanding the big picture, problem solving, and how to break down problems into manageable chunks. We've also discussed the importance of planning. The next attribute that you need to excel at is project scheduling.

A schedule is a required tool for good project management. Scheduling is a mastered art, and very few people do it well. Why? Because it is difficult. In fact, many individuals who schedule projects learned to do so through experience not formal training.

Many individuals who schedule have bad scheduling habits that are very difficult to break. And not breaking these habits can actually lead to significant issues. Why? Because a schedule's outputs are generally accepted at face value as correct. Very few Project Managers actually go into depth and critically analyze their schedules; they just assume that everything is okay. More often than not, however, there are a lot of issues with the schedule, issues that could invalidate key project dates and deadlines.

Properly pulling a project's specifics together in a project scheduling tool is not an easy task. Furthermore, there are many things that you need to understand when it comes to scheduling; these include scheduling basics, guidelines, and best practices.

A step that many Project Managers miss is the assessment of their project schedules against established and proven schedule metrics. The assessment helps identify key schedule deficiencies so that they may be corrected to ensure a more robust schedule. A number of commercial tools are available for this task.

You also need to understand that schedule outputs are deterministic in nature; they always give you the best date based on the information and logic used. But how do you know if the schedule outputs are correct? Many Project Managers rely too heavily on the Critical Path Method (CPM) for the most likely completion date. Most of the time, this results in schedule dates that are inaccurate and optimistic.

To produce reliable results, project schedules should include risk simulation. A proven and beneficial approach is to combine three-point estimation with Monte Carlo simulation. The advantage of this is that schedule targets and the probability of success in meeting these targets are identified and communicated to all project stakeholders.

Since scheduling and costs are related, a similar advantage results for cost targets.

Take time to ask yourself if you are willing to take your project schedule as gospel and commit both yourself and your organization to important deadlines and payment milestones based on its calculations. Ensure that you take the time to thoroughly understand your project schedule, its construct, and the internal logic. Do not assume that the dates that come out of the scheduling tool are always correct and realistic.

HAVE A FIRM GRIP ON YOUR FINANCIALS

Having participated in numerous project reviews, I have seen many Project Managers who, quite frankly, did not understand the financials associated with their projects. This was evident as soon as they stood up in front of a management audience and gave their project brief. After a few questions from the audience, they started to stumble on the financials. Not a good situation to be in.

You need to understand that managing projects is ultimately about managing money. Pure and simple. This applies to private, public, and not-for-profit organizations. As a Project Manager, you are responsible for understanding the financial basis in the makeup of any charges to your project, direct or indirect.

In order to add value to an organization, Project Managers need to understand more than the inner workings of their project. If you do not have a larger financial picture and this broader understanding, you will have difficulty identifying potential project outcomes if problems do occur.

You need to understand, inside and out, how the project's cost file is built up and its associated assumptions. You need to understand what project costs are attributed to what. For example, what are the markups? How do we calculate our costs? Our sell price? Gross margin? How do we calculate fees? What about risk contingency and management reserve? Financials are an excellent and proven way to

35

review project performance. We always want to know how much money we have spent, how much money we have at risk, and how much money we have left. We also need to know how much progress we have made for the money we have spent. This is the basis of earned value management.

From a financial perspective, what happens if you deviate from a plan? Many Project Managers do not take the time to properly address variances, corrective actions, and recovery strategies. Why? Because it's not their money that's at stake. They do not feel accountable for their actions, and generally there are no repercussions. Projects are unique, so there is a tendency to develop a "live-with-it" attitude and to consider this simply a part of doing business. This results in projects failing to meet their goals and ultimately disappointed stakeholders.

One of the fastest ways you can lose credibility in front of management is to not have a sound understanding of your project financials. The minute that management recognizes that you are stumbling, bluffing, or making mistakes, you will lose credibility. So what can you do about it? Well, I am a strong proponent of regular formal project reviews.

Engineers and others in technical or support functions must be conversant with the financial terminology that Project Managers use on a project. They cannot sit on the sidelines and isolate themselves. Everybody needs to talk the same language. Technical expertise on products, projects, service delivery, production, and any other area can be fully harnessed only if others understand the accounting and reporting structure that drives the business.

To get better at handling and understanding project financials, you, as a Project Manager, must insist on timely financial data. Your organization must support you by making financial data available to you in a timely manner. This is a challenge for large projects, where budget responsibilities are broken down into smaller budgets (or segments), each assigned a different manager. I recommend that you make friends in your finance department because, in my experience, finance people have always been supportive. Financial support staff cannot be in the back office. They need to play an important part in the project and participate in it actively.

The bottom line is to never ever leave the financial management of your project to chance. Learn it inside and out. It's so much easier to fix any errors or omissions early on rather than waiting until it's too late. That's when the tough questions begin.

UNDERSTAND YOUR SUPPLY CHAIN

All projects are made up of some type of material, supply, or equipment. An essential element of your success is the timely, accurate, and cost-effective delivery of materials, supplies, and equipment. Supply Chain Management (SCM) represents all activities associated with moving goods from the raw material stage to the final product stage and into the hands of the end user.

Many Project Managers take SCM much too lightly. It is far more complicated than just generating a purchase order or a subcontract for needed items. It involves the production, supply, inventory, transportation, and management of the needed project items. With every step, there is an element of uncertainty, which requires careful oversight and coordination. An issue at any step along the way can easily derail your project.

You also have to take into consideration the return of any defective goods and have a plan in place to ensure your project can accommodate any by-products of this. Depending on the type of project, defects in provided goods can shut down a production line, have significant financial and reputational impacts, and keep your phone ringing off the hook.

The best approach you can use to minimize supply chain issues is to ensure that any goods used in your project have a dual source. You should do your best to avoid any single-cell procurements even though it may not be possible at all times. This is not uncommon in specialized or leading edge technical projects. Depending on the type of project you are managing, a single source may not be allowed. If you have no choice but to use a single-source supplier, ensure that you conduct a vigorous review of the provider.

Successful relationship management of all the suppliers involved with your project is fundamental to on-time delivery. If you or your organization has a bad relationship with one of the project suppliers, it will most likely affect the delivery. And if they are late delivering to you, you will likely be late delivering your project. Remember that suppliers do not *have* to deal with you. You need to make them *want* to deal with you.

Look at it this way. Companies no longer compete against companies. Those days are gone. Now, supply chains compete against supply chains. Imagine that, for one reason or another, a supplier can deliver to only one company. Which one should it deliver to? The answer should be yours! This is why effective supply chain management is critical so that you don't end up in a situation where another company trumped your supply chain as a result of you not managing it properly.

Over the years, I've seen Project Managers blame poor project performance on a supplier or vendor. In doing so, Project Managers use issues with suppliers or vendors as a way of hiding their own performance—clearly they did not properly manage the supply chain. Avoid this trap as it's a clear sign of a lack of accountability-based behaviour.

The key to ensuring project goods arrive as required and with the least amount of grief is for you and your organization to have a solid supply chain management methodology in place. If the project is small enough, then you may actually be the purchasing agent. In many larger projects, purchasing is a separate department, a separate function, and a separate role. Unfortunately, a lot of people have no idea how much management effort is required to get vendors and suppliers to provide what is needed. This is not a trivial task. In fact, the larger the project, the more difficult this becomes.

Transferring risks is a common practice in SCM. Transferring risks involves shifting a risk from one party (you) to another (the supplier). Remember, you may transfer a risk to a supplier, but if the supplier does not deliver, you and your project are still on the hook. Transferring a risk does not remove obligation, and it may have a major impact on you, your project, and your organization if the risk materializes.

A helpful hint is to review and get buy-in on your project schedule from suppliers; then reinforce this buy-in with penalties or incentives. There is nothing more effective than an incentive that goes right to the supplier's bottom line to get the management of the supplier company to pay full attention to you and your needs.

To minimize your risks, ask yourself, do you know all of your suppliers or vendors? How many of your suppliers are single source? Do you know how your suppliers acquire their parts to produce what you need? Do you have the right relationships and, perhaps, the right licenses in place to manage this?

It's so easy to get caught short when it comes to your supply chain. Always remember, it's your project, and you are accountable.

KNOW HOW TO NEGOTIATE

As we all know, negotiating is part of a Project Manager's role. Whether you are negotiating for resources, funding budgets, or facility space, or you're negotiating with subcontractors, vendors, customers, or management, this is just part and parcel of your role. Knowing how to negotiate can make or break a Project Manager.

Negotiation is a process that involves two or more individuals with conflicting positions; the goal is to reach a mutually acceptable agreement by modifying one or both of the original positions. Unfortunately, this definition makes it sound too easy. Knowing how to negotiate properly and in your favour is one of the hardest things you need to be able to do.

There are two main negotiation styles or approaches: *distributive* and *integrative*. Distributive negotiations involve you getting the most out of a situation. This type of negotiation generally deals with a single issue, and both parties are out to get the most for themselves.

Integrative negotiations involve reaching a win-win situation, where both sides benefit. This type of negotiation style deals with more complex issues, and it requires both sides to understand and trust each other. Ensure that you understand both approaches and that you determine which one is the best for you in any given situation. In some cases, you will find that you need to be ready to use both approaches.

There are three key items that you, as a Project Manager, need to address up front before entering into any negotiations.

First, you need to develop a clear picture in your mind of the major project stakeholders. You should already have a fairly good picture of this as a result of your project planning, but reviewing it before going into any negotiations is definitely worthwhile. It allows you to determine (and perhaps update) the influence of the stakeholders and their risk tolerance on your project. More often than not, Project Managers rush to negotiate without a clear understanding of the influence or the risk appetite of the person or stakeholders they are dealing with.

Second, you have to determine your safe zone, or what you can live with after the negotiation is complete. In a simple negotiation, this is a fairly small effort. In more complex negotiations, it will require additional effort and time. Try to keep your emotions out of the negotiation—emotions just cloud the issue. And do not rush this step. What you are determining is the point at which you are ready to walk away.

Third, you must be honest with yourself and identify your trigger points. We all have triggers or pain points, especially when we are under pressure. Trigger points are things that cause you to react strongly, dismissively, with emotion, or just plain rudely. Once you have identified these, work on a plan on how you will react if these trigger points surface in your negotiations. The best approach is to deflect from the point at hand by either asking a question or steering the conversation away from the issue.

Remember, the most important person to know in a negotiation is you.

COMMUNICATE WITH CLARITY

Communication is a broad and multi-faceted term, and an often overlooked, yet critical aspect of project communications is clarity. Achieving clarity is very challenging when it comes to communication. It's much harder than it seems. What clarity requires you to do is to emphasize one specific message at a time. When you are seeking clarity, your aim is to focus on simplicity and precision. Communicating with clarity requires the use of exact, appropriate, and concrete words. It also requires intent.

If you want your project communications to be effective, you must identify the information you want to give and the information you want to receive. If you can communicate with clarity not to one or two individuals, but to a larger group—or perhaps a distributed group if you're working on a global project—you will get noticed. Your credibility will immediately go up as well.

In case you are ever asked to update management on your project, make sure you plan for this ahead of time. Take the time to properly organize and articulate your update. Non-verbal communications are also important to clarity, so you need to get this part right as well. A good message delivered poorly or a bad message delivered well leave two very different impressions. Which one do you think is the winner between the two? Neither. They are both unacceptable.

Project Managers must use clarity in their communications as a tool to gain trust and confidence. Communication isn't about *how much* you say to everyone—it's about saying the right things to the right people at the right time. A lack of clarity can lead to mismanagement and frustration within the project team, not to mention that it's just plain old bad business.

A lack of clarity can also destroy trust depending on which words are used. A simple but poorly worded message, such as an innocent e-mail, presentation slide, or voice mail, may result in an unintentional but major communication breakdown.

Make sure to focus on the types of words you use and to avoid using slang, acronyms, and buzz words. In my experience, these kinds of words (acronyms in particular) tend to have multiple meanings. Also make sure to manage the audience you are communicating with. For live interactions, ensure that you maintain a proper pace that's consistent with your message and that you keep an eye on your tone. Both affect the clarity of your message.

You shouldn't expect clarity in communications from your project team and stakeholders until you incorporate clarity into your own communications. It's up to you to take the first step.

MANAGE YOUR TIME EFFECTIVELY

Here, we find ourselves in a somewhat funny situation. How is it that someone who manages projects and is an expert at planning and scheduling needs help with time management? This is an interesting juxtaposition of ideas, but it brings up an interesting point. Many Project Managers struggle with time management. Want to know why? Because it is hard, and it requires time and effort.

Pressure at work, late supplier deliveries, management poking around, people not meeting deadlines or not taking deadlines seriously—the list goes on and on. Your time always seems to be taken away from you. Project Managers need to learn to properly manage their time in order to properly balance and find time for other activities in life including family, kids, physical activity, and the ever-critical project management training. Many Project Managers decline training because they say they're too busy. Really? The truth is that they're not too busy; they just don't manage their time well, and they aren't driven enough to learn more. I am happy that you, however, are taking the time to read this book!

Your challenges in adequately managing your time are typically caused by a combination of bad habits that don't give you the time you need to properly address your day. Each one of the following habits can take precious time away from your day, but together, they are even worse.

The first deals with planning. Many Project Managers do not take the time to plan out their days properly. Although different Project Managers have different day-to-day management approaches, a daily plan can be a great tool, helping you prioritize your activities and identify your deadlines so that you can focus on the tough, or most urgent ones, first. Make your daily plan first thing when you get to the office, or even better, the day before.

The second deals with micromanaging your team. Work hard to pull back and let your team do their work. Many Project Managers not only micromanage, but also get involved in the work directly, with little or no benefit to the project. This can be very disruptive and damaging to your team. There is no better way to demotivate an employee or a project team than to make them feel like their efforts are continually being scrutinized.

Finally, the third deals with saying NO. Many Project Managers all too easily accept requests for additional project status or unplanned meetings that have no clear agenda and that tend to run long as a result. Remember, it is okay to say NO and to focus on the important things that need to be done.

As part of this, you also need to prioritize your time. As a guide, your first priority is your customer, your second is senior management and its demands, and your third is your team.

You have a lot on your plate and you need to ensure balance. That's where effective time management can be a great help.

REACH OUT

Project Managers have a tendency to try to do everything themselves. They do this because it's easier than reaching out and working with others. In reality, it makes them look weak. You must not be ashamed of reaching out and asking for advice. You should not sit there and stew extensively over a problem. There is a very good chance that others in your organization, or perhaps outside your organization, have had very similar experiences and may be able to help out. You need to ensure you tap into this.

This is where stovepipe organizations come into play. Project Managers need to work around these stovepipes. Unfortunately, we don't always realize we are in one until it's too late. One of the best ways to get beneficial information is to reach across stovepipes and contact individuals who can help you. It is very important to have people around you to reach out to in times of need.

These people may be skilled resources who can provide you with needed information, subject matter experts who can provide guidance, or perhaps just someone to talk to when times get tough. However, if you need to reach out to stakeholders, make sure to do so early on in the project to avoid any last-minute problems. Try not to wait to the last minute to do this, as it may be too late.

Experienced individuals who have the "been there, done that" view can give you tips based on the lessons they learned in the past. You need to find these individuals and reach out to them for their valuable input. You should also reach out to any connections you have with management as they may assist in championing an approach, knocking down project barriers, and ensuring the ongoing success of your project.

In the end, you need to create a network of individuals that you can reach out to if and when the situation calls for it. Don't sit on a risk, issue, or tough problem. Reaching out and seeking advice is often the best way to solve it.

SO WHAT?

As a Project Manager, you have been selected to do an important job. That job is the successful delivery of a project to satisfied stakeholders. Much like successful projects contribute to the overall success of an organization, unfavourable projects negatively impact an organization, exposing it to issues relating to financial performance, legal challenges, and reputation.

Successful execution of your projects requires you to learn and master the attributes of project management expertise. Can you get by executing a project without paying too much attention to the listed attributes? Possibly, but not without great difficulty or sheer luck. And if you do, it is only a matter of time before you fail at a project in the future.

Mastering these attributes will place you in a much more comfortable and powerful position in the future. So why ignore good advice?

PROJECT MANAGEMENT EXPERTISE—DO'S AND DON'TS

Do's

- Take the time to review and clearly understand each attribute. This may require you to do additional research in specific areas, and you are encouraged to do so.

- Actively seek project management training, specifically in project planning, scheduling, and negotiating.

- Join and participate in your local project management community. You will have access to other project managers, events, and information.

- Reach out when you need help. Reaching out is a strength, not a weakness.

45

Don'ts

- Don't lock yourself in your office. Ensure you have an open-door policy and manage by walking around as much as you can. For distributed teams, ensure you check in frequently. Being seen is important to your team.

- Don't single out individuals if there are issues. Ensure you speak with them first.

- Don't ignore risks. Be proactive and transparent.

- Don't believe the project cannot go on without you. No one is indispensable.

KEY CHAPTER TAKE-AWAYS

- Project Managers plan, manage, and handle project details in a way that helps stakeholders relax.

- As a Project Manager, you have the overall accountability for the successful planning, execution, and delivery of a project.

- To be an outstanding Project Manager you need to master the attributes of project management expertise.

- Your reputation precedes you, and your goal is to ensure that it's always positive.

CHAPTER 4: CORE LEADERSHIP SKILLS

Your ability to inspire trust and confidence is vital to becoming a leader and an outstanding Project Manager.

INTRODUCTION

In its simplest form, leadership is about establishing direction and influencing others to want to follow that direction. We hear the term *leadership* quite often, and, quite frankly, it's become a catch-all term whose meaning has been significantly watered down.

With all the leadership information that's available these days, how do you know what's right and what to embrace? What do you really need to know versus what is good for you to know? No wonder leadership is a difficult concept for Project Managers to grasp, to learn effectively, and to practise. It helps to take a step back and look at what is really important to you as a Project Manager.

Leadership is about people. Leadership is about change and causing change. Change affects people. As management is about finding answers, leadership is about asking questions. Part of the reason why leadership has become so important in recent years is that the business world has become much more competitive and full of change.

Leaders develop an ability to anticipate actions and consequences in a way that makes them seem clairvoyant. They have this keen ability to look into the past and into the future. While Project Managers can anticipate things during a project (which is extremely powerful when it comes to risk), leaders can anticipate things beyond a project. They see a bigger picture across the board. They seem to know the right way to approach things, partly due to experience and partly due to their ability to see the bigger picture. The end result is that individuals want to follow them. They see a bright light and someone willing to stand up and go for it.

Individuals want to follow a leader and this is why core leadership skills is a critical component of the Project Management Leadership Model. Individuals want to follow and to be led by an outstanding Project Manager.

WHAT ARE CORE LEADERSHIP SKILLS?

While you may be focused on what needs to be done and may already know how to get the job done, you may not be acting like a true project leader. Let's think about this for a few minutes. You understand the problem, the process, and the steps you have to take. On top of that, you are very systematic in your approach. All of this makes for a good Project Manager; however, it may not make for a good leader. Why? Because people need to be attracted to a leader. They *want* to follow a leader.

Following a leader implies that you are doing so voluntarily. You want to do it. This is a huge differentiator. There are very few things that are more satisfying to a Project Manager than launching or taking over a project and having team members say they admire your leadership and enjoy working with you.

My experiences have taught me that project management leadership is actually a combination of a number of core leadership attributes. Just as we have several attributes for project management expertise, we also have similar attributes for core leadership skills. These attributes look deceptively simple and, in a way, they are because they go back to the basics. However, don't be fooled because they can be difficult to master.

This raises a good question. Do core project leadership attributes have to be complicated? No, they do not. The key is to be consistent in applying them and to fine-tune your approach as you master them.

While the initiatives you face today are challenging, they will be much easier to address if your approach includes the element of leadership. Being a good leader is not complex—you just need to understand and practise the core leadership skills.

With that said, the basic definition of a leader as someone who has willing followers must be expanded to include core leadership attributes, which are based on your ability to inspire *trust* and *confidence*—two elements that are critical to project management leadership success. To be an outstanding Project Manager, your actions must inspire trust and confidence in your project team and in the stakeholders you work with.

The core leadership attributes discussed later on in this chapter are catalysts, or how-tos, that will help you inspire this needed trust and confidence. Without these two things, you will have a difficult time gaining willing followers. And without willing followers, you are not a leader. Keep this in mind as you review and learn the core leadership attributes. *It's all about inspiring trust and confidence.*

WHY ARE CORE LEADERSHIP SKILLS IMPORTANT?

Throughout your project management career, as you progress through the plans, schedules, project reviews, and all those deliverables that kept you up at night wondering if you will make it on time, you will realize that project management is all about people. Without the support of your team, you will not accomplish your project goals. You will fail.

Project Managers who are leaders motivate, challenge, and get the best out of their project teams. They lead their teams to accomplishing great things, and they give others the credit they deserve. The project is not about you; it's about the team, and you're in the background. You ensure a safe environment for ideas and excellence, showing others that anything is possible if they put their minds to it.

Your motivation is fuelled by your vision, and you inspire your team to pursue that vision. It's about having people line up behind you and help you get to your vision. Without your leadership, both your team and your organization will suffer because they will become stagnant and complacent, which in today's world is equal to the death of an organization.

Without your leadership, your project team and organization will struggle to succeed. And if they do not succeed, you will not succeed. As a leader, your job is to make everyone passionate about succeeding.

In today's world, project management expertise needs to be augmented with core leadership skills.

CORE LEADERSHIP SKILLS—ATTRIBUTES YOU NEED TO MASTER

As I have mentioned before, one of things I found frustrating in my project management career is that many organizations struggle with defining observable leadership behaviours that are expected from a Project Manager. As a result, I did not have a firm target to aim for, or my target was frequently modified from assignment to assignment and from supervisor to supervisor. At times, I felt like I was going backward, not forward.

We can simplify this greatly by focusing on the basics. Although numerous models for expected Project Manager behaviours exist, basic issues emerge when you take a closer look at each model. Practicality is one of these issues. These models have to be practical.

As we discussed earlier, management and leadership are often used interchangeably in the project management and business world. They are typically used to depict someone who manages a team of individuals in order to achieve a specific result. However, if you examine this more closely, you will find that it is actually incorrect. In reality, management and leadership have very different meanings, and as a result, they also have very different attributes.

Is there a difference between a Project Manager and a leader? Absolutely there is. Your ability to understand this key point and act accordingly greatly determines your ability to succeed as an outstanding Project Manager. You can increase your success greatly by embracing the attributes discussed in this chapter. So let's review them.

DEMONSTRATE YOUR COMPETENCE

Team members, stakeholders, and management need to feel confident that you are a competent Project Manager. Being competent is not necessarily about being an expert in every area of your domain. Rather, it's about having the proper skills and experience to allow you to make effective decisions.

To do so, you need to make the time to improve your skills continually. Learn how project management is evolving and changing around you. Something that you did five years ago may now have been replaced by a different technique, or perhaps an improved tool, that allows you to approach your current situation in a completely different manner.

As a leader, you need to take the time to study different leadership styles and choose one that best describes you. In my experience, situational leadership—the ability to adapt your leadership style to the situation at hand, based on the individuals involved and the tasks you are dealing with—is an important style to master. This, combined with the management by walking around (MBWA) approach or attitude—as opposed to sitting at your desk or being distant—is very powerful and will greatly help you to succeed. Think of the duo as an unbeatable one-two punch for success.

Ensure that you follow and are active in not only the project management community (such as PMI® Communities of Practice) but also the leadership community. Excellent resources and training programs are available to solidify and broaden your project management leadership skills. This is one area for which I find social media tools such as LinkedIn (©LinkedIn Corporation) and Twitter (© Twitter Incorporated) very helpful. If you configure these applications properly, relevant and useful information will be pushed to you automatically, saving you a lot of time. Participating in relevant leadership groups and following established thought leaders (Kouzes & Posner or Ken Blanchard, for example) are excellent ways to learn and grow.

You need to continually update your knowledge. Don't stand still. Once you master one area, find another. If you stand still, someone will run you over. There will always be somebody who is keener than you are and more aggressive than you are, and they will run you over in your career unless you stay ahead of them. You have to keep your skills sharp and up to date.

An excellent way to do this is take the time to read. For example, you're reading this book. Congratulations! This is an excellent step. I understand you are busy and the last thing you want to do once settled for the day is to open up a book and read about the details of project management. But you need to take the time to do so. It's amazing what you'll learn especially with reviewing case studies. There is nothing more beneficial than understanding other projects and how they overcame challenges.

As a Project Manager, you need to take the time to listen to and learn from subject matter experts. Why? Subject matter experts are exactly that—experts in their domain. Those who truly hold their weight are invaluable to your project. They have gone from project to project, and as a result, they have countless lessons learned that they can share with you.

There is no better way to move your project forward than to consult with subject matter experts. Not only can they assist with technical matters, but they can also help in other areas, especially when it comes to schedules and risks. They know that an activity you think will take only 10 days will actually take anywhere from eight days to 14 days. They understand variability and challenges because they've seen them in the past.

You should also insist on relevant training at work. Once you have had this training, let your employer know that you are willing to take a smaller group of people from your organization and run them through the same knowledge you have just learned. In this way, you are conveying the knowledge that you learned in industry back into the organization. It's a cost-effective, win-win solution that's beneficial for all parties involved.

If your employer will not provide the training, take the time to do it yourself. Somewhere along the line, you may get laid off or lose your job, so you have to be ready for every situation. One of the ways you can prepare for such an event, both from a knowledge and mindset perspective, is to stay on top of your field and remain marketable. Don't lose out to others because you have not had any relevant training over the last five years.

BE CONSISTENT

Being consistent in your actions as a Project Manager is key to establishing yourself as a respected leader who can be trusted. Consistency is an attribute that project teams and stakeholders admire in a Project Manager because they take comfort in knowing who and what they are dealing with. Your ability to be consistent removes a degree of stakeholder nervousness, which is an impediment to progress. However, you need to be consistent in a number of different areas.

When you are consistent, you know your work well, and you approach it with few or no surprises. This allows you to set high expectations for the team without being questioned about your firmness. It leads to higher productivity because it builds momentum. Your team wastes less time trying to predict your actions, and as a result, everyone remains focused. Waffling and changing your mind is very frustrating for those who are trying to work with you.

You also need to ensure that you are consistent when you communicate with team members, stakeholders, and management. This includes all forms of communications and is particularly important when you are dealing with multiple individuals at once. Without a consistent approach, not only will they question your message, but they will also raise questions amongst themselves. Depending on the issue, this may snowball out of control and require significant time—time which you don't have—to rein it back in.

Above all, you have to be consistent in how you treat individuals whom you interact with on a regular basis. Being consistent requires you to avoid sending conflicting or confusing signals to the individuals you are dealing with. Ensure you always treat them with respect, courtesy, and consideration. Be professional at all times, and avoid being moody.

If you are not consistent, you will create confusion, distrust from your project team, and a lack of respect from your stakeholders, management, and even your suppliers and vendors. There is nothing more frustrating than working with a Project Manager who is not consistent.

BE A TEAM BUILDER

Just because you have a group of individuals assigned to you doesn't mean you have a team. So how do you successfully deliver your project when you don't have a team? With great difficulty. Very few things are more frustrating and time consuming than a dysfunctional group of individuals trying to act like a team.

As a Project Manager, you need to be both a team player *and* a team builder. This is particularly important when dealing with a matrix organization. Good team players figure out a way to work with team members to solve problems and get the work done despite their differences. Our agilista friends refer to this as *self-forming teams*. When you build a team and apply the proper leadership, the team will step up, move heaven and earth, and overcome almost any difficulty put in front of it to succeed. This is the type of team you want: one that you helped build.

To build your team, you may need to seek out individuals outside of your current team. You need to be able to recognize people's strengths and potential contributions. This is where your reputation as a Project Manager comes into play. A positive reputation will be a great help in attracting support to your project. People will want to work with you.

The key to building a team is to understand each team member's specific needs, preferences, and style of work. As we all know, everyone has a different style. Your role in building a team is to help people understand their own styles, whether they recognize them or not, and to help them appreciate the different styles of others. Part of your responsibility as a team builder is also being a coach. Your role is to bring people together and help them find the best way to work together.

Do everything you can to build commitment and enthusiasm in your project team. Real power in project management comes from giving and earning personal commitment. Some of the best Project Managers I've worked with were those who actually gave it all they had. They understood that they had issues and challenges to deal with, and they were upfront, honest, and trusting of their team. I was drawn to those individuals, and my gut feeling told me to follow them. Why? Their commitment to the team resulted in such an overflow of positive energy that I wanted to be a part of it.

To be a team builder, you need to show you are committed to the team and its success.

BE AN ACTIVE LISTENER

Often when people talk to each other, they aren't really listening to what's being said. Think about today, the last couple of days, or perhaps this entire work week. How many times did you find yourself sitting in a conversation with someone? Of those times, how many times did you truly listen to the other person and remember the specifics of the conversation? I would venture to say that this number is probably pretty low.

Active listening is a two-way street—it's a structured form of listening *and* responding. You need to listen and respond while giving your undivided attention to the speaker. The way you listen reflects whether or not you want others to interact with you. It is that simple.

Active listening is a very powerful method that you can use to uncover risks and issues in a project. Project Managers must be exceptional listeners. They must be able to Interpret and provide feedback for what was heard. Almost all of the Project Managers I've ever dealt with needed to improve their active listening skills as well as their ability to provide constructive feedback to their team.

Good listeners should pay attention to the person they're listening to, which requires them to be in the present moment, not thinking about the past or the future, or attempting to multi-task or perform other actions while listening. You have to be there, in the moment, and you have to be focused. There is nothing more annoying than trying to have a conversation with somebody who's typing away, writing an e-mail, and talking to you on the side. This is not active listening, not at all.

I understand there are times that call for exceptions to this rule. Urgent things do pop up, and because I promote an open-door policy, I sometimes get interrupted. In these types of situations, I'll say: "If you have an urgent matter do you mind waiting while I quickly finish this e-mail? When I am done, I will focus my attention on you."

I let the individual determine the urgency of the conversation. Working behind closed doors sends the wrong message.

Project Managers must listen effectively because they have to interact and communicate with many stakeholders. However, Project Managers do not always feel comfortable listening to their project staff. This is usually evident in their body language. Why? They do not want to hear the reality because it may reveal a problem or, perhaps, the true status of what's going on. This is where Project Managers get into bad habits like avoidance or ignorance.

If you're sending out a message to your project team and stakeholders that says you really don't want to listen to any tough or bad news, then no bad news will be reported until it's too late. What happens then? You find yourself in a corner because you are accountable for the project. This is one of the key reasons why you have to actively listen. It shows that you have a demonstrated interest in what is going on, and it encourages interaction and transparency.

In the end, active listening results in a higher level of attention, and that's what makes a leader.

ENSURE YOU EMPATHIZE

What is empathy? It's your capacity to recognize someone else's hardships and identify with them. It requires putting yourself in another person's shoes and seeing through someone else's eyes. Empathy is a critical skill for Project Managers. It allows you to better understand your team members as well as their thoughts, motives, perceptions, and concerns. You empathize in order to get a different perspective on a situation. Ultimately, this helps you make decisions.

The beauty of empathy is that team members can learn from you as well. As a result, they actually become better at what they do, and, in turn, help you get better at what you do. Project Managers with empathy do more than just sympathize with the people around them— they use their knowledge to improve a situation.

It is important for Project Managers to show empathy, not just sympathy. Why is this so important? Empathy and sympathy are two different things. Sympathy is simply acknowledging another person's struggles while empathy requires you to truly understand how another person feels especially when it comes to things outside of work.

The key here is to remember that you, as a Project Manager, have a team. Your team members come to work, and they work alongside you every day. But they also have lives outside of work, and sometimes things that happen in these lives will affect their performance on a project. We've all been there at one time or another.

In order to keep your team members on track, you need to get involved in that side of things. By taking the time to get to know them better, outside of the work environment, you will learn to appreciate their cultures, beliefs, and traditions. Take your team out to lunch or a bite after work. You want to have positive relationships with these individuals because they're part of your team.

When you show empathy, you encourage others to follow suit.

ACT WITH INTEGRITY

Integrity is the quality of being honest and having strong moral principles. This is something that I strongly believe in. Strict behavioural adherence to a moral code of some type—reflected in transparent honesty and complete harmony with what you think—is crucial. As a Project Manager, you need to ensure that your behaviours and actions are authentic and based on integrity.

The key in all this is your desire for general good. Morals and ethics, which are a fundamental part of integrity, are all about knowing the difference between right and wrong and about choosing what you consider is right. Acting with integrity means holding true to your beliefs even in the face of serious opposition.

There are a number of behaviours you, as a Project Manager, can focus on when it comes to integrity. Here are a few.

Always tell the truth using simple language. Don't rely on distorted facts, and don't manipulate data or people. Some Project Managers put a "spin" on project reports that makes a situation seem more positive than it really is. You need to avoid doing this. It will catch up with you, and not in a nice way. Do not try to hide or hold back any project information, no matter how bad it may be. Select and use tools and reports that enable you to create project transparency without being forced to do so.

Go out of your way to keep your commitments and deliver what you said you were going to deliver. Not only does this build integrity, but it also builds trust and confidence with others. Integrity is also associated with accountability. A Project Manager who's accountable for a project takes accountability for the end results, good or bad, without pointing fingers at others.

You need to confront tough issues directly and be ready to discuss them honestly, even if your team members or stakeholders don't like your answer. Project Managers with integrity are genuine in their feelings when dealing with others. They are firm, but they do not hold back. They always mean well, they always say what they mean, and they always act accordingly. This results in a mutual respect that is invaluable in the business world.

Project Managers with integrity can be easily distinguished. They have a natural confidence and go about performing their activities with ease while remaining focused on the end results. To be genuine, you need to think before you speak and before you act. You need to gain an understanding of others so that you believe in what you are saying. Think of it as double-checking a situation.

Remember, your team members and stakeholders are always watching. So, if you are consistently displaying these characteristics, they will gladly follow you anywhere.

BE A CONSTRUCTIVE IRRITANT

This is probably one of my favourite terms: *constructive irritant.* As a matter of fact, I consider my main role as a Project Manager to be a constructive irritant. So what is a constructive irritant exactly? Constructive irritants are people who challenge ideas and propose sound solutions. They are consistently seen as better performers by management than individuals who complain about problems, point fingers, and play the blame game while not offering sound advice to the problem at hand.

Constructive irritants are leaders. Constructive irritants challenge colleagues at work. They push back in a constructive manner. They come up with ideas for new products, new services, and innovations even if it's not in their job description. They go beyond what is expected of them. As a constructive irritant, you should question decisions and ask why things are being done a certain way. Your goal is to increase business value.

Being a constructive irritant is a key attribute of being an outstanding Project Manager. While most people follow processes and accept that those processes are just the way things are done, constructive irritants always want to do better. They want to reach beyond what they have now. They want to make a difference.

It's all about knowing the best way to depart from the norm—opinions, standards, and processes. Being a constructive irritant requires a lot of context. You need to understand more than your project—you need to understand the politics of an organization, the key stakeholders involved, and the best way to present your ideas. A constructive irritant focuses on what's right for the project and organization, and this has to be consistent with the organization's broad strategies and objectives.

This means taking your leadership responsibilities very seriously. You need to stand up for what you believe is the best way to move forward and push back when required to do so. You need courage, solid presentation skills, and respect within the organization. You need to consistently leverage common sense in any given situation.

There is a very fine line between being a constructive irritant and a plain old irritant. As a Project Manager, you need to be very careful or people may end up resenting your motives. The key to being constructive is your approach. You need to focus on your style and be sensitive to the audience.

Being a constructive irritant requires having faith in yourself and, at times, having very thick skin.

INFLUENCE OTHERS

Influencing and motivating others, especially in a distributed or global environment, is one of a Project Manager's biggest challenges. Why would somebody want to work long hours and possibly even weekends on a challenging project with you? You need to influence them to do so. This, in turn, increases your strength and confidence as a leader. The end result is increased leadership credibility in the eyes of the project team, stakeholders, and management along with an increased probability of project success. What Project Manager doesn't want this?

Your ability to influence partly depends on the organizational structure of your project. Your ability to influence is much greater when the organizational structure is a strong matrix or fully projectized. In this case, your influence is, in fact, your authority. Having authority does not make you a better influencer, though. Do not confuse the two. If you're working in a weak matrix, your authority is greatly reduced and the reliance on influence increases. In a weak matrix, you must use influence to get things done. There is no way around this. This is where being an effective influencer comes into play. How do you influence without having direct authority over them? Well, you need to be an expert influencer.

Expert influencers influence without authority in order to achieve not only project success, but team success as well. The key to influencing others is how you approach and handle individuals. Influence is invisible. You can't see it or put it on paper because it deals with understanding the way individuals think.

Think about times when you, as a Project Manager, needed support from a functional manager who did not report to you or someone who may have been in a more senior position than you. How did you get these individuals to cooperate with and help you succeed when they had their own issues and challenges to worry about?

Functional managers want to help you, but you need to understand their side of things. Like you, functional managers have

61

many decisions to make and issues to deal with. You need to understand their point of view and make sure that they understand yours. You need to work together to ensure success. How do you do this?

The secret is your attitude. Attitude plays a critical role in influencing to your advantage. You must focus on the success of your project and the success of your team. To do this, you need to be positive and to act like a true champion. You need to be able to clearly explain the benefits of your project and how these benefits help the people you are trying to influence. But first, you must identify these key individuals and develop a relationship with them.

Take the time to understand the work and concerns of these individuals in a personal way. Put away your Blackberry or iPhone. Ask questions to show that you are actively listening. Act with empathy. Discuss their challenges and issues with other individuals or groups to show that you care and want to help them succeed. What you are aiming for is to create reciprocity, a relationship in which each person helps the other.

HAVE THE COURAGE TO ACT

Confidence is key for Project Managers. The ability to get things done in an environment where decisions are difficult to make requires courage. You always need to be ready for a tough decision. You must have the courage to act and to make that decision despite the resistance. Confidence is a mindset that enables you to act effectively when confronted with difficulty, even in the face of fear.

The reality is that we often keep our fears to ourselves. Fear results in anxiety, and it can actually be quite stressful because you don't want to go out on a limb.

So why do you think you need courage? It's because, in business, you often have to make difficult choices in terms of scheduling or even telling a client that his or her delivery deadline is a pipe dream. If you have courage, you are willing to go out on a limb and act because you have faith in yourself and your team. You believe in yourself and in your ability to cope with any given situation. Courage is not about being afraid. It's about working through the fear, remaining calm, and communicating the situation clearly and effectively.

In business, courageous actions are a special kind of risk-taking—it's calculated in the sense that you do not shoot from the hip. You have courage, but you also understand how far to push it and when to stop. Good leaders have a greater-than-average willingness to make bold moves, but they strengthen their chances of success with careful deliberation, preparation, and attention to risk management.

REMAIN CALM

Calm Project Managers are welcome in any organization. They stay calm under pressure. They don't get overly excited. As a result, they tend to focus on what is important, not what is easy. They step back, look at a problem, and know that things are neither as bad as they seem nor as good as they seem.

Calm Project Managers first actively listen, and then they get the facts. They do not overreact. They are even and steady in their responses. You need to stay calm when the going gets tough. Look at the situation you are in objectively. Then sit down and react with a measured, polished, and professional response. You need to determine what is important and deserves your attention versus what can wait to be addressed later. You need to be able to prioritize and act quickly to restore order in a calm manner. By remaining calm under pressure, you can focus in on a problem rather than be distracted by potential outcomes and the blame game.

Believe it or not, some individuals will react in an unsettled manner, by blowing up or throwing their arms in the air, just to create confusion. Unfortunately, this can be frustrating, and it's one of the characteristics of individuals who are intimidated or scared of the situation that they are in. They cloud the situation.

As a Project Manager, you need to work through this. Be careful with people who aren't capable of handling issues calmly, because panic is contagious. Others will start to panic too because that's just the way people react. A calm Project Manager suppresses this.

Every once in a while, you may lose your temper when trying to get things done. The thing that you have to remember in these moments is that blowing your stack is only a short-term solution for your problems. It doesn't help anyone, and it tends to erode your credibility. It doesn't build relationships or encourage a positive working environment. So, there is an overall negative effect.

Keep in mind that you can recover from this, but it takes time.

SO WHAT?

Many of today's project-based organizations are over-managed and under-led. They do not take the time and effort to invest in developing project management leadership as a core of their organization. As a result, they often struggle to succeed in today's challenging business environment.

Successful organizations take a different approach. They don't wait for project management leaders to come along. They invest in and actively seek out Project Managers with leadership potential, and they work with them to develop that potential.

Organizations desperately *want* outstanding Project Managers. They consider this especially important in today's global environment, where Project Managers are not only expected, but required to make more use of distributed teams in order to execute projects successfully.

Project Managers armed with core leadership skills are passionate about their work, and they make it their mission to actively help their team, project, and organization succeed.

Are you up for the challenge?

CORE LEADERSHIP SKILLS—DO'S AND DON'TS

Do's

- Take the time to review and clearly understand each attribute. This may require you to do additional research in specific areas. You are encouraged to do so.

- Conduct a proper analysis of your stakeholders and their influence on your activities. Understanding your circle of influence is key. It will allow you to focus your time and energy where you need to.

- Ensure that you work on developing a situational leadership style combined with a management by walking around attitude.

- Find a senior member of your organization to be your mentor or coach. This person's valuable feedback, insight, and perceptions will help you grow.

Don'ts

- Don't make a commitment you cannot keep. By doing so, you set expectations and cause disappointment.

- Don't interrupt anyone you are speaking with. It's counterproductive, and many people consider it rude. Wait for the speaker to finish.

- Avoid making snap or from-the-hip judgements. It undermines your leadership. Think out your approach after consulting with your team. Let them know how you came to your conclusion.

KEY CHAPTER TAKE-AWAYS

- Leadership and management are not the same thing. Leadership is about people. Individuals follow leaders because they are willing to do so, not because they have to.

- As a leader, you must ensure that your actions inspire trust and confidence in your project team and the stakeholders you work with.

- To be an outstanding Project Manager, you need to master the core leadership attributes.

- Ensure that your behaviours and actions are, at all times, authentic and based on integrity.

CHAPTER 5: RISK-SMART ATTITUDE

Having a risk-smart attitude is critical to project management leadership. Being risk-smart is about understanding the challenges in all your project activities and setting yourself up for success from the beginning.

INTRODUCTION

All projects come with an element of uncertainty. Risk is an uncertainty that has the ability to impact a project. Better defined, it's an uncertain event that, if it were to occur, would have either a positive or a negative impact on project objectives. Although there are many definitions of risk, depending on your source and the business sector you work in, the project management industry has more or less settled on the above definition.

Why don't Project Managers properly plan for risks? Because risk management is generally associated with bad news. Project risks are typically associated with things we don't want to hear, things that are tough, and things that require us to actually give status on events that may impact our project and attract attention—attention we don't need.

However, if project risk management is performed properly—and this is what having a risk-smart attitude is all about—it can be a valuable tool and asset in achieving success. Even though Project Managers now have improved techniques, tools, and processes to help them plan and execute projects well, rarely does everything go according to plan.

Many Project Managers will say that they understand risk management, that they know how to manage risks, and that they have a risk register. They'll tell others not to worry because they have it covered. I have heard this more times than I care to mention. In reality, many organizations and individuals do not understand and properly plan for risks.

With the pressures of business growth, and increased revenues and profit, organizations themselves are not always concerned about risks. They aggressively seek business growth without taking sufficient time to fully understand and prepare for the risks ahead of them. Then suddenly, they find themselves face to face with major issues, issues that could have been avoided.

This type of approach to risk reflects the lack of proper risk culture in many organizations, and it's a trap that you need to be able to recognize and avoid.

WHAT IS A RISK-SMART ATTITUDE?

Project Managers who have a risk-smart attitude are generally much more competent and respected in their work than their counterparts. Many times I've witnessed that Project Managers who are on top of risks within their project and their organization achieve overall greater success than Project Managers who are not.

A risk-smart attitude is all about clear, calculated, and planned actions. It does not rely on any reckless or shoot-from-the hip approaches. A risk-smart attitude involves knowing what you need and asking for it. You must realize that it's okay to ask for advice if you require assistance in assessing or properly responding to a risk. A risk-smart attitude means that you understand the reality of your surroundings, and sometimes this requires you to break the cult of optimism, where others think nothing can go wrong in a project.

Project Managers tend to be very optimistic, and, as a result, they're not fully honest with risks. What you need to do is to make sure that you have a balanced view on risks. Project Managers who have a risk-smart attitude always balance the ups with the downs in any situation. One of the most significant attitude adjustments you can make as you move up the ranks and into upper management is your attitude toward risks and their management. Both need to be front and centre.

Most successful organizations tend to be those where ideas flow freely, but they always have a mechanism in place to make sure that those ideas make business sense. You must learn to take risks in a calculated way. This is what risk management is all about. Having a risk-smart attitude makes it much easier and more effective to do so.

WHY IS A RISK-SMART ATTITUDE IMPORTANT?

Having a risk-smart attitude helps you better understand business value, which is the overall value of a business. Each organization has a different business value because each organization has a different structure and different goals. Project risk management helps increase business value from project investments.

Project risk management increases business and organization alignment as well as general business awareness. It also increases the likelihood of project success. For those of you who work with programs and project portfolios, you know very well that projects are key to implementing strategy and achieving objectives. This also increases business value.

Having a risk-smart attitude is the equivalent of having street smarts. When you are an outstanding Project Manager who has a risk-smart attitude, you just know how to handle yourself when things get fuzzy and unclear. You are able to navigate through any risks, issues and challenges you have in front of you, and you are much more comfortable in doing so.

A key thing to remember is that you can't always be risk-averse. This will be the death of you as a Project Manager. If you're always averse to risks, you will miss opportunities. The proper definition of risk management includes both negative risks (what we refer to as *threats*) and positive risks (what we refer to as *opportunities*). However, you can't always seek risks either. Why? Because you may expose yourself, your project, and your organization to unnecessary risks and potentially serious outcomes. With a risk-smart attitude, you recognize this and ensure that there is a balance between threats and opportunities.

The evolving nature of risks, increased scrutiny from management, and the effects of growing global projects have put extreme pressure on project risk practices. Sarbanes Oxley, better known as SOX, and its Canadian counterpart, Bill C-198, have had a significant effect on publicly traded, project-based organizations. These regulations have been put in place not to be a hindrance, but to help manage and reduce risks as well as to create transparency with proper checks, controls, and balances. The consequences of non-compliance are significant. These regulations are mandated common sense.

As you can see, having a risk-smart attitude as a Project Manager is no longer an option—it's a necessity.

RISK-SMART ATTITUDE—ATTRIBUTES YOU NEED TO MASTER

Just as there are top attributes for project management expertise and core leadership skills, there are risk-smart attributes that you need to master. These attributes align themselves with the attributes from the previous two sections. Understanding and mastering them will greatly help you to become an outstanding Project Manager, to be more successful with your projects, and to achieve both personal and career growth.

Take the time to perform either a literary search or a simple search on the Internet for the term *project risk management*. You'll find literally millions of entries. My last search, taken prior to this book being published, yielded over 100 million entries on Google©.

Most people in the field of project management refer to the PMI® PMBOK® or the PRINCE2® series of documents. Those in IT, use the ITIL®, COBIT®, or the ISO/IEC 27000 series of documents. Many organizations have also embraced ISO 31000 as their guide.

With all these documents and their derivatives, no wonder many individuals end up confused. However, by focusing on and embracing the key risk-smart attitude attributes discussed in this chapter, you are much more likely to succeed.

UNDERSTAND THE BASICS

If you were to review all of the documents listed above, you would find that, while the terms and particularities of each approach may be different, the basics of project risk management are generally the same.

As a Project Manager, you need to understand risk management basics. There is no way around this and no excuse for not doing it, especially since there is so much risk guidance readily available.

The objective of any risk framework is to facilitate the management of project risks by providing structured guidance.

One of the more popular project guidance documents is the PMI® PMBOK®. It's based on a simple yet effective six-step process. Although many guidance and framework documents are available for various industries, the PMBOK® is comprehensive and applies to most projects, most of the time. Figure 5.1, below, shows an alternative view of the PMI® approach.

Figure 5.1. Risk Circle of Life.

I refer to this as the *Risk Circle of Life*, and it serves as a reminder of the following:

- Project risk management is not a supplementary or bolt-on activity. It must be properly planned and integrated into project activities.
- Project risk management consists of six basic steps.
- Project risk management requires open communications and consultation with others.
- Project risk management is a recurring activity. We need to review and update project risks continually, not just at the start of a project.

As you've probably noticed, I have an affinity for circles, and there is a very simple reason for this. Circles are recursive in nature; they keep going and going. In this case, the circle implies that the steps within it must be repeated over and over again if you want to successfully manage risks.

Other standards, methodologies, and processes may have a slightly different approach to risk management, calling things by different names and so on. The general approach, however, remains the same. The basic elements of Figure 5.1 are applicable to the majority of the work you will encounter in your project management activities.

So, with all this information available, why do projects still run into trouble? In some cases, it's because Project Managers have already sold the project to senior management and do not wish to lose support for their project by revealing risks. In other cases, it's due to a lack of understanding of project risk management basics.

MAKE RISK DISCUSSIONS SAFE

One of the reasons why Project Managers shun risks is that they tend to bring bad news. Project Managers hesitate to talk about risks because they are worried about getting themselves into trouble. This belief couldn't be farther from the truth. In fact, if you don't openly talk about risks, there is a very good chance that you will get into much more trouble.

What you need to do is create a safe environment that promotes the discussion of risks. Any idea or proposal that attempts to improve project planning or execution needs to be encouraged, especially if it deals with risks. Creating a safe environment for all conversations is key to receiving important project information in a timely manner. If project team members don't feel safe communicating good news, bad news, or risks, they will delay or avoid doing so. This is the primary cause of surprises. Your team members, stakeholders, and management need to know that sharing these items is okay. Nobody will get singled out at any meeting or in any e-mail for bringing up a risk.

You need to ensure that all participants feel safe working on their project. If they feel safe, the chance of engagement increases significantly. In other words, it's all about people helping people. There is a very good chance that somebody else—within your project, within your organization, or even online in some of the excellent risk-related blogs that you can now participate in—has already experienced the same risk you are currently dealing with.

The goal is to share risk-related information, to get ideas from each other for how to best address risks, and to help the project that you are working on. This means that you have to ensure a safe and open environment. You need to ensure that no bullying occurs and that nobody is called out, made fun of, or spoken to in a negative manner because he or she pointed out a risk. This should apply to all project activities, not just risks.

At the end of the day, the best ideas for addressing risks usually come from others. The only way that you will get those ideas is to create a safe environment for your project team and stakeholders.

LOOK FOR OPPORTUNITIES

As I already mentioned, risks are generally associated with bad news, and thus, they have a negative connotation in most people's minds. This is a great place to start when you first journey into risk management as a Project Manager. Start looking at the threats; understand the basic steps and the mindset associated with identifying threats, assessing them, and responding to them in the best way possible. You also have to ensure that you practise looking for opportunities because not all risks are negative in nature.

The key point here is that a risk may have a positive or negative effect. Unfortunately, many Project Managers tend to think that all risks are negative, that they will actually hurt their project. Interestingly enough, though, risks can be positive in nature and can actually help a project. Understanding this idea fully requires you to shift your mindset.

It's unfortunate that we automatically assume risks are threats because this way of thinking creates a mindset that is a challenge to change. The reality is that risks also represent opportunities, and this is in keeping with today's definition of risk in the project management industry, as discussed earlier. Many Project Managers struggle with this definition, and I've worked with some of them. My recommendation?

For every threat that you encounter in a project, try to also find an opportunity.

Finding opportunities is one area that many Project Managers struggle with. I, too, struggled with it for quite a while until I fully understood the concept of opportunities. Let me explain. First, focus on the term *opportunity.* Ask yourself what you can do to deliver a more successful project. I focus on technical solution, schedule, and cost for starters. Since risk is about uncertainty, I ask myself how I can increase certainty (as opposed to decreasing it when dealing with a threat) in these three areas to ensure success. The best way to do this is to identify the associated risk triggers (the events that cause a risk) and do the best you can to ensure they occur.

Let's use a project schedule as an example. What can you do to increase your success? One way is to ensure you review your schedule in detail and minimize sequential activities the best you can. Can you plan activities in a more parallel manner so that an issue with a single activity does not derail your schedule? Please do not confuse this with determining your schedule's critical path. The single activity may not be on your project's critical path. Pay particular attention to your resources at all times and ensure that your schedule is properly resource-loaded. Also ensure that you have workarounds in place for all your key resources.

One of the reasons why many Project Managers don't look at risks as opportunities goes back to grassroots and the improper use of terms in project risk management. Many Project Managers use the term *risk mitigation* improperly. To me, this is a basic risk management litmus test. Project Managers who say that the risk mitigation strategy for a certain risk is such-and-such are taking the wrong approach.

Risk mitigation is actually just one of four ways that you can handle a threat or negative risk. The others are avoidance, transference, and acceptance. The problem with risk mitigation, when used in a general sense, is that it automatically assumes that you will mitigate the risk even though you have other options. Mitigation may not be the best approach—right off the bat, your mind is biased and you limit yourself.

The proper way to look at risks is to focus on your risk response, and risk mitigation is just one of several possible responses. You need to be aware of this and to use the right terminology. To increase your success, you also need to balance the upside with the downside at all times.

FOSTER A RISK-AWARE CULTURE

Just like you need to make risk discussions safe and promote risk opportunities, you also have to encourage and facilitate a risk-aware culture. This requires everyone in your project and organization to be involved.

How you do this? First, you need to ensure that all participants receive proper risk management training. Using the influencing skills we discussed earlier, you also need to insist that management take at least a summary, if not all, of the same training. In my experience, there tends to be a disconnect between Project Managers, project teams, and the expectations that management has when it comes to risk management. You need to actively address this disconnect.

When you delve into this closer, you realize that most members of management are not trained in the same way and do not understand the same language as you when it comes to project risks. This can cause unnecessary angst and really significant issues during project reviews. To avoid this, everybody who's working on the project, including management, has to have the same training.

The project team and major stakeholders also have to be engaged and assist you in looking for threats and opportunities, even though it may be out of their area of responsibility. Although you are responsible and accountable for all risk management activities in your project, it is not just your job. The project and organization culture has to allow anyone who sees what could be a risk to bring it up with you and anyone else in your organization. Transparency is key.

Proper risk management leads to and breeds success. Risk is about success and unless you have the right culture in place, there is a very high probability that your project and organization will suffer.

ENCOURAGE PROPER RISK-TAKING

One of the key activities a Project Manager should focus on when addressing risk management is to encourage proper risk-taking within the project team. As you now know, you don't want to be overly pessimistic, but at the same time, you don't want to be overly optimistic.

You also have to be sensitive—you don't want too much risk-taking nor do you want too little risk-taking. You can't do this blindly. You need to understand that even though there's no gain unless you try something, you still have to be careful in your approach.

As a Project Manager, you have to know how to push the envelope in a calculated manner. It's healthy to take risks, especially ones that may lead to opportunities. Some of the most successful project organizations today got to that point because they took risks. Rarely, however, were those risks not calculated.

While encouraging risk-taking within your team, you need to ensure that your team members understand why they're doing this in the first place. In doing so, you are encouraging proper and calculated risk-taking as opposed to the shoot-from-the-hip style. Team members who want to try something risky need to have a good reason for it as well as a good idea of the outcome they hope to achieve.

You also need to avoid the big-bang approach to risk responses. If team members identify a risk they want to take, ask them and yourself if there is any way to carry out only a small portion of the risk as a test. Think of this as breaking up the risk and testing it out first. Project Managers struggle with this approach because they do not realize that risk-taking can be divided into smaller steps. However, if properly used, this approach can save you a lot of grief, time, and money.

Make sure that as you encourage risk-taking in your team, you encourage *calculated* risk-taking.

SO WHAT?

Many Project Managers will say that they understand risk management, that they know how to manage risks, and that they have a risk register. They'll tell others not to worry because they have it covered. In reality, the majority of organizations and individuals I've dealt with do not understand and properly plan for risks.

These Project Managers do not consider risk management as value-added work. They perceive risk management plans, risk registers, and risk review meetings as a waste of time. This is, in fact, totally incorrect.

Risks, individually or in combination, have the potential to expose you and your organization to delays and significant financial stress. Ultimately, they damage your reputation and the reputation of your organization. We have seen many situations in the media where organizations have had a black eye as a result of not being able manage risks properly. It is nothing to take lightly.

Failure to understand project risks generally leads to project failure. Having a risk-smart attitude helps you and your project team better understand, plan, predictably execute, and communicate overall project performance. *You have better control, pure and simple.*

Remember that risks must also address opportunities. Not investing the effort to identify opportunities is simply not good business. Developing a risk-smart attitude is one of the best investments you can make.

RISK-SMART ATTITUDE—DO'S AND DON'TS

Do's

- Take the time to review and clearly understand each attribute. This may require you to do additional research in specific areas, and you are encouraged to do so.

- Actively seek project risk management training and ensure management participation.

- Proactively manage and report your project risks. Remember that risk management is an iterative process and must be revisited frequently.

- Carefully review and document your project assumptions and constraints. These may represent significant risk. If not properly addressed, they could lead to a false sense of security and management.

Don'ts

- Don't keep risks and concerns to yourself. Risk management is all about transparent communications.

- Don't focus only on threats. Seek opportunities as well.

- Don't ignore stakeholders, their risks, and their risk attitudes.

KEY CHAPTER TAKE-AWAYS

- All projects come with an element of uncertainty.

- Risk is an uncertain event that, if it were to occur, would have a positive or negative impact on project objectives.

- To be an outstanding Project Manager, you need to master the attributes of a risk-smart attitude.

- The Risk Circle of Life is applicable to a majority of the work you will encounter in your project management activities.

- Project risk management helps increase business value from project investments.

CHAPTER 6: ACCOUNTABILITY-BASED BEHAVIOUR

Accountability involves much more than scheduling a meeting and delegating work to your team. It's about being personally responsible for a project's success or failure and all project activities—good or bad.

INTRODUCTION

Several things contribute to project success and they include a solid project plan, a clear mutual understanding of project deliverables between you and the customer, and, most importantly, the support of the project team as well as any associated stakeholders.

Depending on the size and complexity of a project, many individuals can contribute to and be responsible for it. Front and centre in all this is the Project Manager. Think of the Project Manager as a quarterback of an offensive football team and the people opposed to project changes as the defensive team. I bring up this analogy because I have been sacked a few times in my career. No, not fired, but tackled because my teammates and I did not play as a team.

Have you, as a Project Manager, ever worked on a project that had a disastrous project plan? I'm talking about stakeholders not being properly identified and prioritized, deliverables not being clearly identified, and project requirements not being properly defined. I'm sure you have, much like we all have at one time or another. This reminds me of something one of my old bosses once told me, "Laszlo, these types of projects build character. Consider the alternative." What this person really meant to say was "Get it sorted out, Laszlo, or you'll lose your job!"

As I diligently worked on getting the project back on track, I realized that neither my project team nor my management understood the importance of accountability in a project's success. While I had no problem with being accountable, I noticed that no one else on my team felt the same way. So, I quickly realized that I needed to make the project team and stakeholders feel the same way I did. Basically, if a project team does not embrace accountability-based behaviour, the chances of success are greatly reduced.

You may be wondering if there is a difference between accountability and responsibility in project management. Most definitely, yes! Unfortunately, many individuals I've dealt with do not understand this difference.

WHAT IS ACCOUNTABILITY-BASED BEHAVIOUR?

Accountability, like risk, is such an important part of being an outstanding Project Manager that it makes up its own, separate component of the Project Management Leadership Model.

In today's business world, accountability and responsibility tend to be used interchangeably, much like management and leadership. I have seen this countless times. But, is there a difference between accountability and responsibility? The answer is yes! And you need to take the time and effort to understand this difference.

Responsibility, on one hand, focuses on what an individual can or should do. When used in the context of a project, it defines the ability and obligation of an individual or team to accomplish an activity. Accountability, on the other hand, is about an individual or a team meeting set expectations and accepting the consequences if they do not meet those expectations. The difference between the two is like the difference between black and white. In your mind, there should be no confusion between the two terms.

Although accountability is a desire, it is often not the reality. Accountability-based behaviour requires Project Managers to be actively accountable for all activities that they are involved in. It focuses on achieving results rather than just doing the job. It doesn't hide project failures, challenges, setbacks, and risks; instead, it seeks solutions to move the project forward in a positive manner.

Accountability is all about establishing a clear direction for the project team with clear expectations and non-negotiable priorities.

WHY IS ACCOUNTABILITY-BASED BEHAVIOUR IMPORTANT?

Have you ever managed a project in which members of the project team did not directly report to you? It's safe to say that all of us have worked in a matrix-like organization at one time or another—I have many times. Ideally, you want to have strong control over your project team versus little control over it—this is the difference between a strong and a weak matrix.

In many organizations, Project Managers are accountable for the success of a project, but they do not have direct authority over their staff. This is increasingly common these days as more and more people work on multiple projects at the same time in order to keep project costs down.

So how do you effectively manage project resources when you do not have direct management authority over them? If your team members do not report to you, how can you have authority over them? This can be a very difficult and frustrating situation, especially since you remain accountable for the project. You are stuck in the middle.

Project team members who consider themselves *responsible* help you only part of the way. These individuals have no issues doing their job, but they generally don't respect your schedule or expectations. Furthermore, when a tough issue arises, they tend to hide behind processes, or lack of processes, and start passing the buck. Most of them do not feel liable for the completion of their assigned tasks.

On top of this, your ability to such resolve staffing issues could be severely limited because your position in the organization may not be senior enough. Being an expert influencer helps, but you may have to rely on other members of management to help you sort out the problem. It may seem as though your project is headed for a very steep cliff, and the end result may very well be project failure. This is not a good place to be as a Project Manager.

In contrast, project team members who see themselves as *accountable* provide a totally different picture. It's a great picture. It's like a breath of fresh air. Although the project reporting structure has not changed, team members now personally take ownership of their assigned tasks and understand the consequences of not meeting expectations. In a lot of cases, they also take it one step further—they help each other if need be. They want to succeed. They want you to succeed. They want the project to succeed.

Accountability-based behaviour plays a critical role in project success. Without it, most projects are likely to fail. Depending on their complexity and size of the project, the failure may come with major financial, organizational, and reputation repercussions.

ACCOUNTABILITY-BASED BEHAVIOUR—ATTRIBUTES YOU NEED TO MASTER

Much like the first three components of the Project Management Leadership Model (project management expertise, core leadership skills, and risk-smart attitude), the fourth component, accountability-based behaviour, has several attributes you need to master.

All of these attributes align themselves with those of the previous three components, and they generally cover all the bases associated with accountability-based behaviour. As always, Project Managers are encouraged to do more research on this critical subject because understanding and mastering the attributes will catapult your career as an outstanding Project Manager.

SET CLEAR EXPECTATIONS

A critical step in ensuring that project staff and stakeholders respond in an accountable manner is to clearly identify what is expected of them. Individuals need to know what is expected of them so they know what to aim for.

Setting clear expectations can be a difficult challenge for Project Managers. You can't waffle or hesitate. Any expectations that you set need to be clear, concise, and relate easily to the project. They must be clearly understood both by you and by other project staff.

Expectations need to focus on performance and not process. Individuals may hide behind processes and use them as an excuse for their performance. Project team members tend to be very capable; if they have to figure out how to do something, they will. This is why you have to focus on performance and deliverables rather than the process and motions. A bonus is that issues with the process will be flushed out.

IDENTIFY NON-NEGOTIABLE ITEMS

Non-negotiable items, in the context of project management, are things that must occur when they're expected to occur. Good examples of this include firm delivery dates, a financial profit or gross margin goal, or perhaps the launch date of a new product.

It's up to you to identify your project's non-negotiable items and to make sure that your team members understand that they must meet these expectations—that non-negotiable items are set in concrete. To avoid confusion, team members and their managers must have a clear understanding of what these non-negotiable items are so that they can communicate clearly amongst themselves as well as with other individuals involved with the work. This ensures an aligned approach.

TRACK AND RESPOND

Now that you have set clear expectations and have identified your non-negotiable items, you have to ensure that you have a process in place to monitor and track your project's progress against those items and that you respond (some people prefer the term *react*) if required to do so. You have to ensure that expectations are turned into actions and that they are tracked frequently, openly, and with everyone.

If your expectations and non-negotiable items are not met, you have to take prompt action and address the issue with the individual or the team. As a Project Manager, you cannot simply say "Oh well!" and let it pass. This is one of the worst things you could do. What's more, your team will catch on very quickly and not care about future expectations. In order to hold individuals accountable, you have to call them out on their actions when they do not meet expectations or non-negotiable items. And it's important to be consistent in this area.

FOSTER AN ENVIRONMENT OF NO EXCUSES

From what I've seen in my experience, many individuals like to pass the buck. They like to hide behind processes and behind a lack of clarity, using these things as an excuse for why things did not go according to plan. And I can see why—many times there are no repercussions of doing so.

Accountability-based behaviour requires you, as a Project Manager, to reject excuses. Sure, sometimes things come up, and you have to adjust—it's understandable as long as there's a valid reason for it. If something doesn't get done, you must clearly identify the reason why, make sure it's valid, and move on.

Do not accept excuses that involve bad behaviour, interpersonal staff issues, hiding behind processes, and a general lack of will to get the work done. Accountable Project Managers do not accept blame. In other words, one individual cannot blame another individual in the project team.

The reason why something didn't get done has to be factual. More importantly, you have to ask your team, did you work together to try to fix this? If the answer is no, then it's your responsibility to communicate to everyone that this type of behaviour will not tolerated. Working together and helping each other is a necessity. This needs to be part of the project culture.

Team members have to understand that the rules have changed. They can no longer shrug things off, and there are serious consequences to not meeting expectations and non-negotiable items.

ENSURE SELF-ACCOUNTABILITY

So far, we've discussed a number of key attributes. It's now time for you to walk the talk. In other words, all the items we just talked about also apply to you. Project Manager behaviours that enforce accountability on everyone but themselves are not acceptable.

Your actions speak very loudly, so if you don't pay attention to the same things you've imposed on your project team members, they will notice, and they will likely do the same. You'll likely end up being asked, "That was okay for you but not okay for us?" As a Project Manager, you have to avoid this situation by always doing what you said you were going to do. Don't just hold your staff accountable—hold yourself accountable as well. Be a leader. Be an outstanding Project Manager.

SO WHAT?

A lack of accountability has become the cultural norm in many organizations. To succeed, project-based organizations must embrace, promote, and enforce an accountable culture. Much like successful projects support the success of an organization, accountability-based behaviour does the same.

A project that does not have clear expectations and non-negotiable items has no leadership. A project that doesn't have consequences for unmet expectations and non-negotiable items has a high probability of failure. Lack of both personal and project accountability also encourages non-performers to thrive while the a few select individuals always pick up the slack. It makes for an uncomfortable and stressful environment.

Accountability-based behaviour helps you overcome this and achieve outstanding results.

ACCOUNTABILITY-BASED BEHAVIOUR—DO'S AND DON'TS

Do's

- Take the time to review and clearly understand each attribute. This may require you to do additional research in specific areas, and you are encouraged to do so.

- Set and communicate project expectations and non-negotiable items clearly. Make sure they are clearly understood by your project team.

- Encourage your team members to help each other if they come across any issues.

Don'ts

- Avoid passing the buck and blaming others. You need to walk the talk and set an example for the rest of the team.

- Do not waiver on your expectations. Be positive but firm when dealing with your team.

- Avoid accepting excuses for set expectations not being met.

KEY CHAPTER TAKE-AWAYS

- Accountability and responsibility tend to be used interchangeably, but there is a significant difference in their meaning.

- Responsibility focuses on what an individual can or should do.

- Accountability refers to an individual or a team meeting set expectations and accepting the consequences of not meeting those expectations.

- Accountability-based behaviour requires Project Managers to be actively accountable for all activities that they are involved in.

CHAPTER 7: PULLING IT ALL TOGETHER

The most important part of being an outstanding Project Manager is the ability to understand how the individual areas of the Project Management Leadership Model integrate with each other and work together.

INTRODUCTION

We have now reviewed the four components of the Project Management Leadership Model, which is meant to help Project Managers focus on what is important, not what is easy. Easy is what our bad habits represent.

The model is meant to act as a reminder of and guide to the basics that Project Managers need to master if they want to excel in their field and become outstanding Project Managers. We have reviewed all of the components and attributes that make up the model, and we have covered a lot of ground doing so. Congratulations on making it this far!

WHAT WE HAVE LEARNED

To be successful, Project Managers must break away from bad habits that impede their road to success. Unfortunately, they may not even be aware of these habits.

The Project Management Leadership Model is composed of four basic yet key interacting areas, which represent good, solid habits. They are habits that we want to focus on. Let's review what we've learned.

- Project management expertise: Knowing how to plan, manage, and handle details in a way that lets others relax
- Core leadership skills: Having a vision, sharing it with the project team, and then setting the course using your ability to inspire trust and confidence
- Risk-smart attitude: Honestly understanding and accepting the reality of your surroundings and where you are now
- Accountability-based behaviour: Having a willingness to openly accept the consequences for something you have done or something that you're supposed to do

All of these are key drivers in the model, and all of them are necessary to becoming an outstanding Project Manager. You cannot be an outstanding Project Manager unless you master these four areas, nor can you be an outstanding Project Manager without being aware of and actively participating in the four areas at any one time. Being good, or even great, in just one area is not enough. The approach is not singular. All of these components need to be developed and practised at the same time.

The intent of the model is to show Project Managers what needs to be addressed. It is meant to be a guide, helping you in your personal and professional development.

THE COMPLETE MODEL

As mentioned above, the Project Management Leadership Model is made up of four components and includes a total of 31 individual attributes, each one tied to the other. When all of these are pulled together, the model looks like Figure 7.1.

Project management expertise

1. Understand the big picture.
2. Recognize a good requirement from a bad one.
3. Be able to analyze and break down problems.
4. Know how to plan.
5. Excel at scheduling.
6. Have a firm grip on your financials.
7. Understand your supply chain.
8. Know how to negotiate.
9. Communicate with clarity.
10. Manage your time effectively.
11. Reach out.

Core leadership skills

1. Demonstrate your competence.
2. Be consistent.
3. Be a team builder.
4. Be an active listener.
5. Ensure you empathize.
6. Act with integrity.
7. Be a constructive irritant.
8. Influence others.
9. Have the courage to act.
10. Remain calm.

Risk-smart attitude

1. Understand the basics.
2. Make risk discussions safe.
3. Look for opportunities.
4. Foster a risk-aware culture.
5. Encourage proper risk-taking.

Accountability-based behaviour

1. Set clear expectations.
2. Identify non-negotiable items.
3. Track and respond.
4. Foster an environment of no excuses.
5. Ensure self-accountability.

Figure 7.1. Complete Project Management Leadership Model.

The first thing that should strike you as you look at the model is its simplicity. It represents common sense in project management. That's the whole premise of this book, and that's what drives the model. It's all about going back to the basics and understanding their critical importance.

The second thing you should see is that the attributes under each component are linked. They are not isolated; rather, they support each other and work together. Improving on one will help the others as well. Similarly, if you let one slip, the others will follow suit.

WHAT'S NEXT? STEPS TO HELP YOU GET STARTED

One of the advantages of the Project Management Leadership Model is that it doesn't follow a serial approach like a number of other models out there, which take you from left to right, step by step, with each step building on the previous one. This model and its approach are not about passing any gates to reach success. They're about focusing on what is required for success.

Many Project Managers are at different levels and stages of their project management careers. Some of you are just starting out in your careers, others are transitioning to project management after mastering other fields, and others still are seasoned veterans. The great thing about this model is that it's meant to help you succeed no matter where you are in your project management career—because we could all use a refresher every now and then in our career journey.

All components and attributes discussed in this book have been identified in such a way that you can work on them in parallel. Refer to Figure 7.2. This is why risk-smart attitude and accountability-based behaviour are separate components of the model. You need to recognize and focus on them so that you are armed to make a difference early on. I've noticed that these two are items that we delay addressing, learning about, and getting better at for two reasons. First, it's hard to do. Second, the items are not emphasized as a key part of project management knowledge. The end result is that many individuals do not honestly consider them essential components of a Project Manager's tool box. This needs to change.

The key of this model is to work on improving your mastery of the components in a parallel manner. Be patient, though, because it does take experience and time to get things moving forward. The important thing is to know what to expect as a Project Manager and to be ready. That is an incredibly great and satisfying feeling.

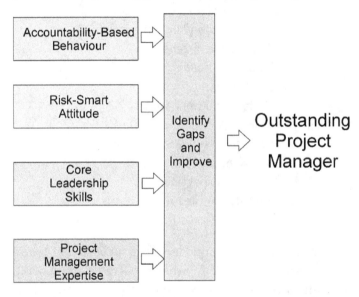

Figure 7.2. Parallel Approach of the Project Management Leadership Model.

In a perfect world, I would ask you to address each one of the components and attributes at the same time (and if you can do this, great!). The reality is, however, that it can be quite challenging. To help in this area, I recommend focusing on certain areas first. This doesn't mean that these are the only areas to focus on, but they do allow you to get started more easily, especially if you are a junior Project Manager or new to project management. Alternatively, you can also sit down with your supervisor, peers, mentor, or coach and seek advice from them based on your current situation and strengths.

To guide you along your way, I've highlighted the three key areas of each component of the Project Management Leadership Model. Focus on improving in these areas first.

- Project management expertise:
    - Understand the big picture.
    - Communicate with clarity.
    - Reach out.
- Core leadership skills:
    - Demonstrate your competence.
    - Be an active listener.
    - Be a team builder.
- Risk-smart attitude:
    - Understand the basics.
    - Make risk discussions safe.
    - Foster a risk-aware culture.
- Accountability-based behaviour:
    - Set clear expectations.
    - Identify non-negotiable items.
    - Ensure self-accountability.

We have taken four components and focused on 12 attributes. These attributes are very powerful when used as a starting point. Beginning with and focusing on these now will make a huge difference later on in your future as a Project Manager.

YOUR ROAD TO SUCCESS IN PROJECT MANAGEMENT LEADERSHIP

These are exciting times in the discipline of project management. Everyone is facing significant challenges, and these will become even more demanding as the world changes around us. With the growth of global projects, there are also opportunities for outstanding career growth.

Being an outstanding Project Manager also brings about an opportunity that most people do not think about. Later on in life, many of you will likely become business owners, and your experience in project management will be invaluable. The discipline, management, and leadership practices you learn while becoming an outstanding Project Manager will go a long way in helping you run a business. Being an outstanding Project Manager is a great way to learn how to run a business.

You are now armed with the basics that will make you an outstanding Project Manager. I recommend that you continually review your progress using the model. Take the time to adjust where it's required. Ensure that you take your career seriously and with conviction. Reach out and ask for help when you need it. Remember not to get bogged down. All of this is part of your journey to achieving project management success.

CHAPTER 8: PROJECT MANAGEMENT LEADERSHIP ASSESSMENT

Now that you understand the components and attributes of the Project Management Leadership Model, you need to evaluate yourself using the model and to identify opportunities for improvement.

INTRODUCTION

Now that you reviewed the material in this book, you need to complete a detailed assessment of your current performance using the Project Management Leadership Model. To help with this, I have created a detailed assessment form for project management leadership. The form is based on the model's components and attributes.

As we discussed in Chapter 2, the detailed assessment form is designed to baseline your current performance and to allow you to track your improvements with periodic reviews in the future. It may also be used by others you have chosen to evaluate your performance. Having someone else evaluate you is highly recommended for maximum effectiveness of this model. What you see and what the other person sees may be significantly different. If so, you need to determine why. Using the model will help you do this.

HOW TO ASSESS YOURSELF

The detailed assessment form is not complicated. In fact, filling it out is simple and straightforward. You rate your performance for each component and attribute in your day-to-day work on a scale of 0 to 5 (outlined in Table 8.1 below). Be honest with yourself and ensure that you can provide specific examples in the comments section to support your scoring. Include your information in Table 8.2.

Table 8.1. Scoring System for the Project Management
Leadership Detailed Assessment

Score	Criteria
0	Attribute is not practised.
1	Attribute is rarely practised. Needs significant improvement.
2	Attribute is somewhat practised. Needs major improvement.
3	Attribute is practised. Needs improvement.
4	Attribute is frequently practised. Monitor and adjust.
5	Attribute is mastered.

Table 8.2. Project Management Leadership Awareness Detailed Assessment (Page 1)

Project Management Leadership Detailed Assessment Chapter 3 Project Management Expertise		
Attribute	**Score** (0 to 5)	**Comments**
Understand the big picture		
Recognize a good requirement from a bad one		
Be able to analyze and break down problems		
Know how to plan		
Excel at scheduling		
Have a firm grip on your financials		
Understand your supply chain		
Know how to negotiate		
Communicate with clarity		
Manage your time		
Reach out		
Total	/55	
Score (equal to the total above)	**/55**	

Table 8.2. Project Management Leadership Detailed Assessment
(Page 2)

Project Management Leadership Detailed Assessment Chapter 4 Core Leadership Skills		
Attribute	**Score** (0 to 5)	**Comments**
Demonstrate your competence		
Be consistent		
Be a team builder		
Be an active listener		
Ensure you empathize		
Act with integrity		
Be a constructive irritant		
Influence others		
Have courage to act		
Remain calm		
Total	/50	
Score (equal to the total above)	**/50**	

Table 8.2. Project Management Leadership Detailed Assessment (Page 3)

Project Management Leadership Detailed Assessment Chapter 5 Risk-Smart Attitude		
Attribute	**Score** (0 to 5)	**Comments**
Understand the basics		
Make risk discussions safe		
Look for opportunities		
Foster a risk-aware culture		
Ensure proper risk-taking		
Total	/25	
Score (equal to above total X2)	**/50**	

Table 8.2. Project Management Leadership Detailed Assessment (Page 4)

Project Management Leadership Detailed Assessment Chapter 6 Accountability-Based Behaviour		
Attribute	**Score** (0 to 5)	**Comments**
Set clear expectations		
Identify non-negotiable items		
Track and respond		
Foster an environment of no excuses		
Ensure self-accountability		
Total	/25	
Score (equal to above total X2)	**/50**	

Table 8.2. Project Management Leadership Detailed Assessment
(Page 5)

Project Management Leadership Detailed Assessment Total Score		
Component	**Score**	**Comments**
Project management expertise	/55	
Core leadership skills	/50	
Risk-smart attitude	/50	
Accountability-based behaviour	/50	
Project Management Leadership Assessment Total Score (Total of components scores)	/205	
Project Management Leadership Assessment Final score (equal to Total Score/205 x 100)	**/100**	

Now that you have completed the detailed assessment, you need to review how you did. Your goal is to reach a minimum score of 4 for each attribute for a total score of 164 of a possible 205. This corresponds to a final score of 80 out of 100, or 80 %.

ASSESS YOUR PERFORMANCE REGULARLY

Please do not try to slice and dice the results or determine other mathematical ways of doing the assessment. This is not the point of the assessment. There is no pass or fail. It's about recognizing which project management leadership components and attributes you need to improve on to increase your level of performance.

Three things are important to remember:

- Each attribute needs to be practised, not skipped or overlooked. These attributes represent the basics.
- Each of the four components must be practised in parallel. Using the scoring approach of Table 8.1, a final score of 80% corresponds to each attribute being frequently practised. This means that you are actively monitoring your performance and are adjusting your actions to improve at each level. This is what you need to strive for, and it's the main goal of the detailed assessment.
- Ensure that you assess your performance regularly. I recommend you do this every six months at least or when you start a new major assignment or job. To help you track your progress, keep a journal of your detailed assessments and include any notes or comments. This is an excellent method of capturing any lessons you may have learned on your journey.

A key lesson I have learned over the years is that seeking constructive feedback from others is invaluable. Many individuals I have worked with tend to get defensive when they receive feedback; my advice to them is don't be. The key is to listen for, identify, and take away the key nuggets that will help you improve. The true mark of success is constant self-improvement, which is the result of a strong desire to bring out the best in yourself and to help others along the way. This is true project management leadership.

CHAPTER 9: ITEMS TO GUIDE YOUR DEVELOPMENT

INTRODUCTION

You now know the requirements of the Project Management Leadership Model and what it takes to become an outstanding Project Manager. You have assessed yourself against the model and are now ready to put your knowledge to work. Becoming an outstanding Project Manager will not happen just by reading this book. Turning the ideas in this book into actions and continually improving against the self-assessment criteria will, in time, make you an outstanding Project Manager.

Now that you have completed a detailed assessment of your current performance using the model, you need to take the time to develop a plan for how you will improve in the areas you have identified. To help with this, I have compiled a list of techniques and recommended reads, which I believe will be of benefit to you. You are encouraged to review these and to add any other items you find helpful during your journey.

TECHNIQUES TO DEVELOP PROJECT MANAGEMENT EXPERTISE

- Understand the big picture:
    - Use an Executive Project Summary approach to briefings. All projects can be placed in a diagram on a single page.
    - Identify all the major stakeholders and perform a thorough stakeholder analysis.
    - Research your organization's past and future plans.
    - Attend internal networking events (Lunch and Learns, after-work events, etc.).
    - Ask questions.

- Recognize a good requirement from a bad one:
  - Understand the characteristics of a good requirement.
  - Do not mix user, system, and design requirements.
  - Ensure that requirements are realistic.
  - Avoid a requirement that imposes a solution.
  - Ensure that all requirements are verifiable.

- Be able to analyze and break down problems:
  - Learn to apply structured problem-solving techniques.
  - Identify the root cause of the problem to clearly understand it. Use the 5 Whys approach.
  - Don't rush into solutions. Take the time to find the right solution.
  - Encourage your team members to participate. They may see a problem in a way you do not, or they may have solutions you have not thought of.
  - Look at multiple solutions and their trade-offs.

- Know how to plan:
  - Break down the work using a Work Breakdown Structure (WBS) approach.
  - Review and document all project constraints and assumptions.
  - Plan in detail only as far ahead as is sensible at the time. Break down your plan into phases or stages.
  - Clearly define your deliverables and the acceptance criteria for each.
  - Involve your team in the planning process to get their buy-in.

- Excel at scheduling:
  - Seek training in this area. It will be invaluable.
  - Don't start scheduling without creating a plan first.
  - Understand scheduling best practices and know how to create a proper Critical Path Method (CPM) schedule.
  - Move tasks that are difficult or involve risks closer to the start of your project. Avoid low-hanging fruit.

- o Incorporate schedule and cost risk analysis where possible.

- Have a firm grip on your financials:
  - o Understand what drives your project, your business, and the bottom line.
  - o Understand the figures—they belong to you, so you are accountable.
  - o Learn the difference between contingency and management reserves and ensure these are in place.
  - o Clearly understand cash flow management and ensure your cash flow remains neutral or positive.
  - o Make sure your finance team is made aware of all major risks and issues as well as of their potential impacts on both the project and the organization.

- Understand your supply chain:
  - o Take time to learn about supply chain management and its various components.
  - o Identify and establish a relationship with the people who will be supporting your project's supply-chain needs.
  - o Do not bypass your buyers or your delegated supplier interface when you have an issue. Work together to avoid confusion and delays.
  - o Ensure your project schedule has a contingency plan in case of late deliveries to your project. Request more frequent updates as critical delivery dates approach.
  - o Do your best to avoid single-source suppliers.

- Know how to negotiate:
  - o Seek training in this area. It will be invaluable.
  - o Find a mentor or coach with whom you can practise and fine-tune your style.
  - o Always prepare for negotiations.
  - o Think outside the box. There may be several ways to get what both parties want.

- o Do not be afraid to invite an objective third party into the discussion. He or she may have new ideas.

- Communicate with clarity:
  - o Learn to summarize key ideas. Use the summary to recap and check your audience's understanding of the material.
  - o Include a thorough stakeholder analysis in your project communications planning. Ensure you understand what, when, and how stakeholders wish to communicate.
  - o Leverage both push and pull methods of communicating. Push for what is time sensitive or requires action. Let other information be pulled by stakeholders in an agreed-to manner.
  - o Schedule time every day to proactively communicate with your team.
  - o Ask for feedback on your style and approach.

- Manage your time effectively:
  - o Develop a daily plan based on what you have going on that week.
  - o Set goals for the week and place them somewhere visible so you can see and remember them.
  - o Avoid multi-tasking if you can. Focus on the requirement at hand.
  - o Apply the 80/20 rule. Don't just work smart, work smart on the right things.
  - o Insert a daily 30 to 60-minute administration slot in your schedule for time to yourself.

- Reach out:
  - o Develop a network of people to whom you can reach out in times of need.
  - o Encourage team members and peers to do the same.
  - o Offer to help others and share your experiences with them. Ensure that this is a two-way street.

- o Reach out to the project management community by networking with other Project Managers using social media or by joining a project management group.
- o Keep a database of lessons learned and share it with others.

TECHNIQUES TO DEVELOP CORE LEADERSHIP SKILLS

- Demonstrate your competence:
  - o Continuously read up on and keep abreast of project management knowledge, leadership developments, and related news.
  - o Participate in project management and leadership webinars.
  - o Get involved in the project management and leadership communities.
  - o Participate in relevant leadership groups and follow established thought leaders.
  - o Apply for and present at project management conferences.

- Be consistent:
  - o Think about the long term, not just days or weeks.
  - o Balance optimism and reality.
  - o Don't shoot from the hip. Think things through first.
  - o Never make a commitment you know you can't keep.
  - o Understand the link between your work and the organization's strategic goals.

- Be a team builder:
  - o Celebrate team success publicly.
  - o Keep your attitude positive and your motivation levels high.
  - o Don't say anything negative that could damage team morale.

- Listen to ideas and suggestions from your team members and make it clear that you're always available to help.
- Use praise more than criticism and leave room for team relaxation and fun.

- Be an active listener:
  - Keep an open mind to what you are hearing.
  - Face the speaker and maintain eye contact.
  - Wait for the speaker to pause if you want to ask questions. Do not interrupt.
  - Ask clarifying questions, not challenging questions.
  - Pay attention not only to words, but also to feelings, facial expressions, gestures, posture, and other non-verbal cues.

- Ensure you empathize:
  - Learn to identify your own feelings so you can relate to others better.
  - Understand your bias and how it may affect others.
  - Regularly ask others for their perspectives and/or feelings about a situation.
  - Avoid making snap conclusions.
  - Control your emotions.

- Act with integrity:
  - Be honest with yourself and with others.
  - Be genuine and transparent with others.
  - Treat others with respect and candour.
  - Live up to your standards and always do the right thing.
  - Ensure you are grateful in your surroundings.

- Be a constructive irritant:
  - Be realistic.
  - Get a second opinion on any new ideas.
  - Challenge your colleagues at work in a positive manner.
  - Seek practical solutions to challenges.

o   Aim high. Go above whatever your role says you must do.

- Influence others:
  o   Identify and review your circle of influence.
  o   Understand the influence and authority that others in your circle have.
  o   Build and nurture an environment of trust.
  o   Improve your communication and presentation effectiveness.
  o   Narrow down and focus on important things that you need controlled.

- Have the courage to act:
  o   Improve your communication and presentation effectiveness.
  o   Be realistic.
  o   Understand the situation and its risks.
  o   Recognize if your motivation is personal or organizational. Act for the proper reason.
  o   Get a second opinion before making any decisions.

- Remain calm:
  o   Recognize warning signs of excessive stress at home or work.
  o   Reduce home and job stress by taking care of yourself.
  o   Recognize and effectively use non-verbal cues and body language.
  o   Focus on the good (even when things are bad).
  o   If you're feeling flustered, take a moment to cool down before sending any e-mails or leaving any voice mails. Come back to them once you've calmed down. It may save you from doing something you'll regret.

TECHNIQUES TO DEVELOP A RISK-SMART ATTITUDE

- Understand the basics:
  - Develop a risk management strategy for your project.
  - Have clear definitions for impact, probability, and risk severity for all stakeholders
  - Balance risk management effort and cost with benefits.
  - Pay attention to other people's biases and tolerances.
  - Keep track of and review lessons learned.

- Make risk discussions safe:
  - Put risk discussions on the agenda for all major meetings.
  - Listen to your team.
  - Always be positive and ask questions.
  - Treat people with respect and professionalism.
  - Do not be confrontational.

- Look for opportunities:
  - Use a risk-severity matrix that includes both threats and opportunities.
  - Ensure that for every threat you identify, you also identify an opportunity.
  - Where possible, minimize sequential events in your project.
  - Review project constraints and assumptions. These may represent significant risk.
  - Reach out and ask others for input—it may save you a lot of time.

- Foster a risk-aware culture:
  - Communicate openly about risks.
  - Follow up on any risk-related actions and lead by example.
  - Organize a Lunch and Learn on risk.
  - Openly appreciate those who bring forward new ideas.
  - Find and distribute risk-related articles.

- Encourage proper risk-taking:
    - o Make sure everyone understands that benefits need to outweigh the drawbacks.
    - o Use decision-making tools to help you analyze risks.
    - o Always reward success.
    - o Emphasize that there is no such thing as failure as long as you can learn from your mistakes.
    - o Seek management support when necessary.

TECHNIQUES TO DEVELOP ACCOUNTABILITY-BASED BEHAVIOUR

- Set clear expectations:
    - o Determine your organization's overall direction and objectives.
    - o Identify project deliverables and their owners.
    - o Be specific and descriptive.
    - o Ask questions to ensure your team completely understand the project.
    - o Hold regular performance reviews and seek feedback from others.

- Identify non-negotiable items:
    - o Insist on respect, honesty, and professionalism.
    - o Identify critical project events, deliverables, and owners.
    - o Post items in a public, well-travelled area.
    - o Ensure frequent and open communication with everyone involved in the project.
    - o Raise the bar and push the team to achieve it.

- Track and respond:
    - o Establish an open-door policy.
    - o Review and communicate the status of your organization's goals.
    - o Hold frequent informal discussions and reviews.

- o Provide status updates to your management.
- o Do not stand still when faced with an issue. Take swift action.

- Foster an environment of no excuses:
  - o Look out for excuses and remind your team that they are not allowed.
  - o Discourage procrastination.
  - o Challenge difficulties in order to help create opportunities.
  - o Create a positive mindset.
  - o Lead by example.

- Ensure self-accountability:
  - o Review priorities and non-negotiable items with your team and management.
  - o Be transparent.
  - o Do not belittle or down talk to anyone in or outside of work.
  - o Review your status frequently and adjust as required.
  - o Walk the talk.

RECOMMENDED READINGS

I make it a point to continually look for and read books that will help further my understanding of project management leadership. In fact, reaching out to and following up with a number of the authors has resulted in friendships that I greatly cherish to this day.

Of the books I have read, the following are my top recommendations for improving your project management leadership knowledge:

- *Project Management: A Systems Approach to Planning, Scheduling, and Controlling*, Harold Kerzner PhD (John Wileys and Sons)

- *Effective Project Management: Traditional, Agile, Extreme*, Robert K. Wysocki (Wiley Publishing)
- *Business Driven PMO Setup: Practical Insights, Techniques, and Case Examples for Ensuring Success*, Mark Price Perry (J. Ross Publishing)
- *Business Driven Project Portfolio Management: Conquering the Top 10 Risks that Threaten Success*, Mark Price Perry (J. Ross Publishing)
- *Business Driven PMO Success Stories: Across Industries and Around the World*, Mark Price Perry (J. Ross Publishing)
- *The Leadership Challenge*, Kouzes and Posner (John Wileys and Sons)
- *Leadership Agility: Five Levels of Mastery for Anticipating and Initiating Change*, Bill Joiner and Stephen Josephs (John Wileys and Sons)
- *Good to Great*, Jim Collins (Harper Business)
- *Leadership: Theory and Practice*, Peter G. Northouse (Sage Publications)
- *Practical Schedule Risk Analysis*, David T Hulett PhD (Gower Publishing)
- *Integrated Cost-Schedule Risk Analysis*, David T. Hulett PhD (Gower Publishing)
- *Identifying and Managing Project Risk: Essential Tools for Failure-Proofing Your Project*, Tom Kendrick (American Management Association)
- *Simple Tools and Techniques for Enterprise Risk Management*, Robert J. Chapman (John Wiley and Sons)
- *Making Yourself Indispensable: The Power of Personal Accountability*, Mark Samuel (Portfolio Penguin)
- *Creating the Accountable Organization: A Practical Guide to Improve Performance Execution*, Mark Samuel (Xephor Press)
- *Cowboy Ethics: What Wall Street Can Learn from the Code of the West*, James P. Owen (Stoecklein Publishing & Photography)

117

THE TRUE MARK OF SUCCESS

As mentioned in Chapter 8, the true mark of success is constant self-improvement, which is the result of a strong desire to bring out the best in yourself. Although I have provided techniques and recommended readings to help you get started and improve your performance, it does not stop here. You need to develop your own journal based on the experiences you gathered and the discoveries you made while applying the model.

To help you track your progress, keep a journal of your initial and regular detailed assessments and include any notes or comments. Keep track of techniques that you have found beneficial. List and summarize the literature you have read. Take time to save key points from relevant webinars, groups, and practice communities you are following. Reflect on any feedback you have received from others and pull out those nuggets that will help you succeed.

Committing to and keeping a journal of your progress shows that you understand the significance of investing in what is important—yourself.

ACKNOWLEDGEMENTS

Over the years, I have had the pleasure of meeting and working with a number of individuals who have provided me with the ideas, guidance, and inspiration that have become the backbone and construct of this book.

During this entire process, I learned that you must not underestimate who you meet and the insights they offer. It may not be obvious at times, but we all have something to offer, and we need to learn to open our hearts and listen. To these individuals and their powerful lesson, I remain forever grateful.

I am particularly grateful for the following outstanding individuals who helped with the creation of this book. Their insights, feedback, and support were invaluable, and I truly value their friendship.

- Larry Johnson
- Mark Price Perry
- Mark Samuel
- Ron Guidinger
- Gerry Bush
- Derek Hughes
- Melanie Mitchell
- John Alsop

Mark Price Perry (www.botinternational.com), Mark Samuel (www.impaqcorp.com) and David Hulett (www.projectrisk.com) have written books that have positively shaped my thoughts on various aspects of project management. Reference to these excellent works is made in Chapter 9 of this book.

And to my beautiful wife, Lisa, and wonderful boys, Andrew and Alexander—thank you for putting up with me during all this. I love you all dearly.

Laszlo

NOTES

Notes

Notes

Notes

CPSIA information can be obtained
at www.ICGtesting.com
Printed in the USA
LVHW041604300519
619610LV00013B/605/P